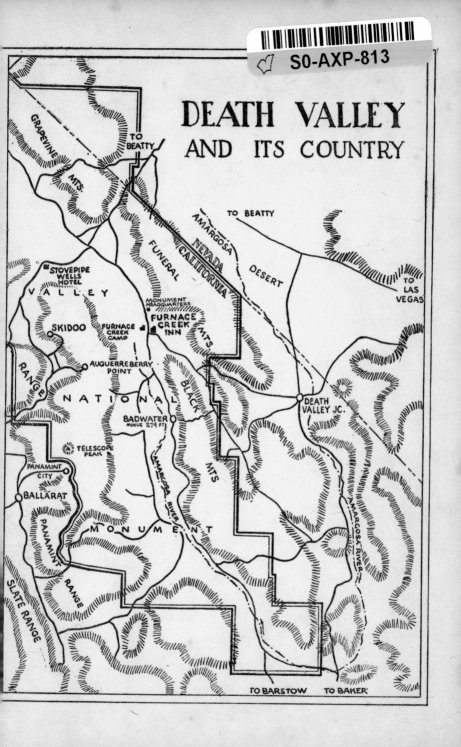

DEATH VALLEY
AND ITS COUNTRY

Death Valley and its Country

BY GEORGE PALMER PUTNAM

The Southland of North America

In the Oregon Country

Andrée, the Record of a Tragic Adventure

Soaring Wings, the Biography of Amelia Earhart

Wide Margins

Duration

DEATH VALLEY
and its Country

GEORGE PALMER PUTNAM

DUELL, SLOAN AND PEARCE
New York

To

"T. R."

Superintendent of

Death Valley National Monument

who has done so much for

the Valley and its

friends.

Contents

Death Valley and its Country

1. The Valley

MOST fabulous of the desert places of America is Death Valley, sultry and surprising, seen first by white men only a brief hundred years ago.

The geologic story of the world's creation is recorded there as nowhere else. Superlatives cling to it. Once called the deadliest sink, to be avoided at all costs, now it is the most visited, although with the scantiest permanent population.

As well, it is the lowest, driest, and hottest place in America. It is so hot scorpions die in the sun, yet in the tourist season its prize view is best reached on snowshoes. It has the continent's newest land and the oldest. The first survey party used camels, and it was Chinese coolies who leveled a roadway across its salt flats.

More improbable facts are true, and more fantastic falsehoods are told, of Death Valley than of any other like region.

It has a "castle" that cost well over a million dollars, scores of miles from the nearest habitation, supposedly financed with gold from a mine no one ever saw. There are mountains of borax, beds of solid salt eighteen hundred feet thick, streams that become smaller the farther they flow, lakes that dried up a million years ago, sardines pickled in brine that coyotes eat, fossil tracks of elephants and camels, super-heated winds that bring ducks down dead if not roasted, frogs that sing scales, hills that move when the wind blows.

In the region today there are no railroads, but some impressive depots where railroads used to be; one is a bar, another a school, a third a dance hall, and the fourth a home, with the ticket window opening between kitchen and living room.

The local phenomena also include aborigines of sorts, a metropolitan resort hotel, complete with swimming pool, landing strip, and golf links, some of the weirdest scenery in the world, and a legendary character called Death Valley Scotty.

Scotty's incredible biography figures later in this volume, together with some account of his Alice-in-Wonderland abode and the wonderful yarns he will tell you there. His tales have all the flavor of the bizarre land where this modern Munchhausen lives.

One night as we sat in the patio of Scotty's palace, a feminine tourist turned wide eyes toward our host.

"Oh, Mr. Scott," she twittered, "you have saved *so* many lives here on the desert, won't you *please* tell us one real story of your heroism?"

Scotty scratched his head. "Well, lemme think—"

"How about the old couple that were lost up Sure Death Canyon?" I suggested.

"Them? That warn't nuthin'." Scotty grunted and shifted in his chair. "Well, I wuz out prospectin' when I come across an old man an' woman. They'd driv up in their auto an' th' damn thing had broke down. They hadn't et or had a drop o' water fer two days. Must've bin all of a hundred and fifty miles from anywhere.

4

"Well, I only had my burros, but I give 'em what water and grub I had an' started back to git help. Then I got to thinkin'. Time I got back them two would be dead. An' they'd sure have suffered to beat hell. Took me quite a spell to figger out what to do."

Scotty stopped.

"Oh, Mr. Scotty," the woman begged, "what happened?"

"Went back an' shot 'em!" Scotty wiped his eyes. " 'Twas th' only Christian thing to do."

Best known of the aborigines you may see is Johnnie Shoshone, an ancient Indian who serves as primitive adornment for the tourist trade. This venerable dean of his people is, among other things, a master of the retort accurate.

In the days after a Civilian Conservation Corps had camped in the Valley, sometimes creating other things besides fine roads, a visitor noticed a red-headed Indian child and asked Johnnie about it.

"Half breed?" she inquired.

Johnnie shook his head.

"Half CCC," he said.

It was Johnnie who happened on gold where the Montgomery-Shoshone mine was born at Rhyolite in 1905, launching that boomingest boom town, the last of the breed in the Death Valley country. Bob Montgomery gave Johnnie a pair of fine new overalls and two dollars. Johnnie put his mark on a paper which gave Bob his rights of discovery.

About five million dollars was taken out of that mine, and some might contend that the Indian was treated badly. But I think in the long run Johnnie probably felt all right about it. In less than five years Rhyolite was dead. Johnnie wasn't. The desert moved in again. The wealth of Rhyolite disappeared. Its buildings crumbled. The white people, with their strange

5

ways, left. But Johnnie, who had his overalls, stayed on where he and his people had always been.

Death Valley's famous hotel is an oasis of luxury called Furnace Creek Inn, uniquely situated at sea level, its urban elegances out of all proportion to its altitude. A mile away, beside a date grove, is the less pretentious Furnace Creek Ranch.

It was along Furnace Creek Wash, in 1849, that the first white tourists camped, emigrants with their ox-drawn wagons seeking a short-cut through the wilderness of unknown deserts to California's golden El Dorados. Their tragedies, high courage, and mistakes are an epic chapter in the story of Western pioneering.

Somewhat later—April 27, 1866, to be exact—one R. H. Stretch delivered this journalistic blast: "Life on Furnace Creek would be infinitely more unbearable than a sojourn in State Prison."

It would be interesting if the spirit of that dismal reporter could revisit the place today. Or if the shades of the stricken members of the Manly party could see from the Beyond the prodigious modern conveniences that prevail where once they ate their oxen and struggled on afoot.

Within sight of Furnace Creek are fanciful samples of the scenery which makes Death Valley what it is. Rounded hills and low cuestas of clay and ash, of pink and green, brown, gray, yellow, and white, fringe the Valley's salty floor. Some of the giant cones of clay, vanilla-and-strawberry colored, are capped with burnt rock, a powdering of lava for all the world like chocolate sauce atop gargantuan sundaes.

One of the Valley's show places is called Dante's View. But that specialist in hellish scenery could scarcely equal what went on in this California country in the eras when the present geological formations were being created. Even today, its internal fires cooled, Death Valley remains a reasonable facsimile of a first-class Inferno, in a state of suspended animation.

Some of the old mining camps, now only ghostly remains, were pretty hell-roaring, too. Panamint City was the wickedest.

A tale of Panamint concerns the mirror that was freighted at great cost from San Francisco to adorn the most handsome bar any mining town then boasted. It was a mirror whose elegance and sumptuous proportions staggered the local imagination, even the more legendary because it had already traveled from France by way of Cape Horn.

Each day, riders and stages brought to the camp advance bulletins of the mirror's slow progress by freight team. For twenty-two days the treasure crept closer, while preparations for its reception occupied the community. That reception was to make all other celebrations pale, insipid, and puny.

Came the great evening. As soon as the mirror had been installed by a hundred eager hands the festivities got under way. Toasts were drunk, and more toasts, and after that, what better way to admire the new acquisition than to line up at the bar and watch your hand carrying a glass to your lips? The citizens of Panamint cooperated so wholeheartedly in this pastime that by morning some were the least bit belligerent. To the tune of tinkling glass, the mirror, shattered by a hundred bullets, crashed into oblivion.

There is another small tale which gives the flavor of the elder citizens, whose spirits are somewhat less inflammable. It also concerns the christening of a new bar, to which important social event a character called Old Man Halsey was invited.

From his desert claim Old Man Halsey sent one of his non-descript Indians the seventeen intervening miles with his R.S.V.P. which said: "Can't make it. Hen going to hatch."

A few days later another message arrived: "Perhaps can come. Four eggs broken."

The night before the celebration a stolid emissary brought a final postscript: "Count me in sure. Cat ate chicks."

The western wall of Death Valley is the Panamint Range, for which the mining camp was named. Not so long ago (after all, the whole span of the region's recorded history is scarcely a century), those mountains provided a favorite hideout for citizens who had killed carelessly or decamped for graver reasons like appropriating a claim, a horse, or a woman. It was a standing jest that the mail for such absentees should be readdressed care of the Panamints.

Actually, a spring of water on the fringe of Panamint Valley, near the attenuated shade of some mesquite, came to be called Post Office Spring. Letters for those in temporary retirement were left there, in an RFD box of sorts made from a packing case with a slanting hinged roof, set up on a couple of stakes.

In that brash era the law's sense of humor perhaps was more subtle than today's. I have in mind a brawl in the course of which one undesirable shot another, not fatally, but very painfully. The two were locked in the same cell by a pragmatic sheriff who felt benefit to the community might be derived. But it didn't work out. Neither's throat was cut, for both men managed to stay awake all night.

Five hundred and fifty square miles of Death Valley proper, which is some one hundred and fifty miles long and twenty to twenty-five miles broad from crest to crest of the enclosing

8

mountain ranges, is below sea level. Badwater, the lowest point on the continent, with a minus elevation of 279.6 feet, is less than eighty miles on a direct line from Mt. Whitney, 14,496 feet high, the highest peak in the United States. From near Dante's View you can see both the *top* and the *bottom* of America.

Telescope Peak, rising 11,045 feet from the sub-sea-level floor of the Valley, is the *tallest*, if not the highest of American mountains, for its altitude is gained all in one visible gesture.

Among the environs of the Valley as well named as any are the Funeral Mountains which fringe the Valley on the east. I do not know who named them, or when. But as early as 1866 they were thus described in the Virginia City *Enterprise*: "The Funerals are frequently capped with heavy masses of black limestone or basalt, the debris of which, running down their slopes, gives them the appearance of being fringed with crape, a species of natural mourning." In Death Valley, even the hills wear weeds! Rounding out the lethal nomenclature, there are Coffin Canyon, Skeleton Mine, and Dead Man's Gulch, as well as Hell Gate.

The Amargosa River, which, in the Southern California pattern, is a considerable stream during the brief rains and a trickle of dust at other times, first flows south and then in a giant geographical contortion turns due north, finally disappearing entirely among the salt beds that pave the central portion of the lowest sink.

This kaleidoscopic introduction to Death Valley, like first impressions of the place itself, may have some element of breathlessness. At least its rambling indefiniteness has much in common with the Amargosa River—and both end where this book begins.

2. The Name

O_N the map you will find Death Valley
located in the eastern part of California adjoining the Nevada
boundary, two hundred and fifty miles northeast of Los Angeles, and on the arid, inland side of the Sierra Nevada Mountains. Today, with all its remoteness and its harsh past, it is
a region of good roads, comfortable resting places, and easy
access.

The lure of its attractions is indicated by the fact that during its six-month "season" from November first to May first,
over a hundred thousand visitors came to the Valley proper.
For a resort whose permanent summer population is less than
thirty, that is an impressive pilgrimage.

On February 11, 1933, Death Valley was made a National
Monument by proclamation of President Hoover. Its area was
set aside to be maintained in its natural state as a perpetual
public property, administered by the National Park Service,
which functions as part of the Department of the Interior.

A Monument differs from a National Park primarily in that
it is created by presidential proclamation, whereas a Park
10

requires an act of Congress. Parks are mostly associated with outstanding scenic beauty, or as sanctuaries for the propagation of wild life, or a combination of the two. Monuments are usually places of historic or geographic interest, unique on a smaller scale than parks.

Forest Reserves—of which there are several throughout California, Death Valley Monument's nearest neighbor being Inyo National Forest on the west flank of Owens Valley—are administered by the U.S. Forest Service of the Department of Agriculture. Forest Reserves, like the Parks, are held for the public use but their economic resources are employed commercially under governmental supervision, whereas the Parks are preserved as nearly as possible in their natural condition, their grazing kept for their native animal population.

Incidentally, in Death Valley, the men with the straight-brimmed Stetsons and olive-green uniforms are called *Park* Rangers. A *Forest* Ranger is a member of the Forest Service personnel.

Although most of Death Valley National Monument is in California, it now includes a small section in Nevada, brought in by President Roosevelt in 1937.

On the west the Monument is rimmed by the Panamint Mountains; on the east by the Grapevine, Funeral, and Black Mountains. The Last Chance Range pinches out the northern end of the Valley, and the Avawatz and the Owlshead Mountains block it at the south.

The Monument exceeds in size (2980 square miles) all National Parks in the continental United States except Yellowstone. Its distinctive types of scenery, its geological phenomena, its flora, fauna, and climate are not duplicated in any other of our National Parks. Or, indeed, in any of the desert regions of the Southwest, if one regards its dramatic quota in the aggregate.

11

Death Valley Monument itself is nearly twice the size of Delaware. At that it comprises less than a third of its own outsize county, Inyo. And Inyo County is larger than any one of eight states; is larger than Connecticut, Delaware, and Rhode Island combined; is larger than Massachusetts.

Death Valley was given its name when the first white travelers, seeking gold, struggled through it in 1849. At least, that is the traditional story which has persisted and been embroidered on from time to time.

The beginning of the story is to be found in the pages of the Valley's chief source book, written by William Lewis Manly who was a young man when he crossed the Valley with a pioneer expedition, and an aging man, some forty years later, when he wrote his informative journal, *Death Valley in '49.*

In that retrospective record Manly wrote: "Just as we were ready to leave we took off our hats, and then overlooking the scene of so much trial, suffering and death spoke the thought uppermost saying, 'Good-bye, Death Valley!' Then we faced away. . . . Ever after . . . it was called Death Valley."

It may have happened exactly that way in 1849. But it is no unkindness to entertain a measure of skepticism about events long remembered, for the romanticism of memory readily can blur the focus of exact facts.

For instance, even the Manly story has several versions. One of them is to be met right at Furnace Creek Inn, stated positively by Johnny Mills, an authentic old-timer who first came to the Ranch in 1896 and has been thereabout ever since. Mills says he talked with Mrs. Bennett, another member of the expedition, when she revisited the Valley in her later years. He says her story then was that before they left their starvation camp on the floor of the Valley there were prayers, and possibly some singing, and *she* gave the place the name

12

"Valley of Death." All of which is not mentioned by Manly.

The divergent memories are of historical interest because they illustrate how even the chief figures in the story disagree as to factual details.

Manly himself contributed evidence which casts an interesting sidelight on the subject, though before this no one seems to have noted it. In the Huntington Library is the original sketch Manly drew, showing the Jayhawker party's route leaving Death Valley. When he wrote in place-names on that sketch he called it "White Valley"—a title quite appropriate to its gleaming white salt flats. True, on another sketch in the same collection he did use today's accepted name.

But at least such discrepancies and this retrospective vagueness furnish fuel for the theory of some who feel that it was the Indians themselves who originated the name which came to be applied to the valley they once called Tomesha, or "ground afire." They believe that the idea of death and the place Tomesha were linked for centuries in the Indian order of existence.

North of the Sand Dunes in the upper central part of the Valley once were Indian camps. Artifacts, potsherds, and petroglyphs, as well as good water are in the immediate area. The ancient community located there in the heart of the hot flats may well have functioned as a health resort of a kind. The comparative mildness of the winter climate compared with the chill, high country roundabout, and the therapeutic baking of summer, made this a curative refuge for the ailing and the aged.

Many who were brought there died. Naturally, it became a residence of death, too, in the minds of those who used it, so that the Indians came to call the place the valley of death.

As recently as thirty years ago there were old-timers who talked about such things. They remembered how the sick were carried there and how the old died. And some of them, at least, felt that its name was a heritage of the natives who lived and died in Death Valley.

Charlie Walker is an old-timer who believes the Indians probably used the name Death Valley long ago.

"Those were permanent camps where the Indians lived up on the slopes not far from Stovepipe Wells," he says. "And you know, if anyone died, the survivors would move away. That's because the spirit of the dead person was supposed to come back and plague the survivors. It would have been a great nuisance to give up whole camps when people died, and they were dying all the time. So whenever some one was sick or very old, he was moved down to the pleasant warm places on the floor of the Valley and fixed comfortable there and left to die. Sure it was Death Valley, all right."

With the Indians, death in the Valley was wholesale.

While there was hardship a-plenty for the white men, death laid its hand lightly on the first visitors. There is a measure of confusion in what has been written about those early days and in the evidence remaining from the pioneers themselves. Not a single grave in all the Valley marks the resting place of any member of that original party whose many deaths—and only one of them actually recorded by Manly—are supposed to give the reason for the Valley's naming.

T. R. Goodwin, superintendent of the National Monument and a Death Valley enthusiast steeped in its lore, believes that this one death is the only authenticated tragedy of that trek of 1849, despite all the lethal literature that has been written about it.

In his book, *Here's Death Valley*, C. B. Glasscock, who knew so well this desert and its history, declared that the only member of the '49 party who perished in Death Valley itself was "Captain Culverwell, who died at the foot of the Pana-

14

mint slopes near Bennett's Well." Which substantiates Manly's record of a single death.

There was reason for those pioneers to look back and call the vale they'd struggled through Hard Times Valley, or Hungry Valley, or Thirsty Valley—or as Manly himself at least once called it, White Valley. But that December of 1849 it was not a valley of death. In no winter has there ever been any hazard of heat, or even critical lack of water for those conditioned in desert ways. The tribulations of the pioneer parties resulted from ignorance, poor planning, inadequate equipment and supply, coupled with the fact that they and their animals were worn in body and spirit from the long, hard road already traveled for eighty weary days.

Someone *did* first use the words "Death Valley." It is a resounding phrase. Anyone would like to coin it, or be credited with its creation.

There is nothing conclusive about these observations. Their essence, I suppose, is that there wasn't any considerable dying that year the name was supposed to have been bestowed, while for many, many years before, natural death and the Indians and the Valley were an inseparable triumvirate.

3. "They Died of New Boots"

WHEN and by whom ever christened, Death Valley it is. By any other name its story would be as fanciful and its mortality as high.

In the later years, death visited the Valley often enough. Sometimes its passage was well recorded, sometimes obscurely, and now and then it was linked with rememberable fragments of human history.

A score of graves mark where prospectors and strays perished. Not many died of heat. Brawls and liquor contributed their share, for mining was a dour business, camps tough, and the Panamints peopled with characters who found it healthy, for reasons often associated with homicide, to retire temporarily from the legal entanglements of society.

Natural death came to at least one wayfarer by drowning. In that instance there is no question as to how a geographical name originated, because when Ben Stewart was making topographic maps in 1895 he encountered the body of a man where a cloudburst flood had washed it, at the bottom of a then-nameless gorge. There was a letter in the dead man's

16

pocket. His name was Titus. So was Titus Canyon christened.

In a more modern way, and upon a larger scale, death visited Death Valley again on August 1, 1944. Flying from Army fields not far distant upon the deserts, two B-24 bombers collided at some 20,000 feet directly over the main salt flats west of Badwater. Seventeen of the eighteen men on the two planes were killed. A tail gunner, a youngster on his first considerable training flight, was thrown free and parachuted to safety.

Over on the eastern fringe of the Valley, among the canyons of the Funeral Mountains, a remote echo of tragedy was passed on to me by Frank Grace, who for thirty of his seventy years has prospected and mined in those hills.

We sat in the mouth of one of the tunnels he has put through the solid rock with his own labor alone, every powder hole made with his single jack, one hand striking with the hammer, the other holding the drill. Beside us was a canteen of water, an ancient skillet for panning gravel, a sack of dynamite sticks, a pile of ore samples, and some canvas pack-sacks of high-grade he would carry down two miles over steep trails to the end of the road he had made himself across the wash.

A notice was penciled on a piece of board propped up on the shabby bellows. It read:

> *Please dont take anything*
> *someone stole the rope off*
> *my hoist bucket he wore rubber*
> *shoes and came in a jeep*

My host saw me reading the notice, which under the circumstances seemed very temperate.

"Yeah," he said. "I did some tracking. One day I'll catch up with the bastard. It's a long way to tote stuff up here to have someone steal it."

17

He was silent for a space, looking out where the hot bare hills showed lavender beyond our shaded resting place. Sitting there framed by the handiwork of a hard lifetime, he came to speak, as so many do, of death in the Valley, remembering especially the case of Alfred Nard, who is buried down below where we talked. Death caught up with the tired man on his hot way westward from Rhyolite to Skidoo.

"Likely he died of new boots," said Old Man Grace. "That was pretty common."

Which it was, if one chose summer travel over broiling deserts with new boots. Feet swell and sweat. The new footgear becomes unbearable. Once the shoes are shed, bare feet, soon blistered and cut by stones, are a hard added handicap, often enough fatal.

"It was new boots that done it all right," Grace continued. "There was nothing to tell where he came from. Someone just happened to know his name, over in Rhyolite where he'd worked as a cook.

"When I heard about him having been a cook, it set me thinking back to a time up at the old mill below the Keane-Wonder Mine. While I was waiting there one day I got to looking through some Western Federation of Miners papers. Well, some lady back East, Philadelphia I think it was, had a notice asking for information about her son, who'd disappeared. Nard was his name. She said he was a cook.

"So I went back to the mill and tried to find that paper. Thought I'd like to tell the mother, but this paper was gone. Likely someone burned it."

Old Man Grace was silent for a space.

"Well, the desert ain't a bad place to be dead in," he added meditatively, looking out upon it from the mouth of that tunnel a third of his lifetime had gone to make.

18

Charlie Walker, too, is near seventy. With Pete Auguerre-berry, Shorty Harris, and Chris Wichts gone, there aren't so many of the old-timers left, at least not still mining.

A while back Charlie found a deserted camp in a little canyon tucked away below Sheepshead Mountain.

"It looked like a first-class murder mystery," said Charlie. "There were dishes still on the packing-box table, though squirrels and such had eaten the food. A catsup bottle was half full. Cans of codfish and corned beef stood around. Tent poles were standing, though the canvas had blown away. Bedding was on the two cots, there was a pillow on the ground, a riding saddle sitting on a rock and even the miner's best friend, a Dutch oven, with the heavy lid in place, had a hunk of half-cooked bread in it. The whole setup looked like the folks just disappeared without expecting to at all."

I said it sounded like the *Marie Celeste* mystery, and Charlie agreed.

"Only this one was solved," he said.

"How come?"

"Well, I spent two days hunting around those canyons for the bodies. I thought sure there was at least one murder. There weren't tracks, so I knew whatever happened, happened a long time before. In the dry air, of course, the bedding and canned stuff would last almost indefinitely. Even if coyotes had eaten the body, I counted on finding bones. But nary a bone."

Months later Charlie was sitting in a restaurant in Beatty.

"Someone had asked me if I ever found those bodies. As I told him no, I hadn't, a big man came over to my table.

" 'Bodies hell!' he said. 'That was my camp.'

"Then that galoot sat down and told me all about it. He and his partner had been run out of Skidoo. They laid low for a time in that canyon. Then one day all of a sudden they decided to light out for Rhyolite, to try their luck a bit at faro, and come right back. Their luck was too good. In just one night they cleaned up a nice pile and never did go back to camp.

" 'We was too rich to bother with chicken feed like that,' the guy told me. I remember how he came back to where I was sitting after he'd started to the door. 'An' Mister,' he said to me, 'my wife wants that Dutch oven.' "

Charlie ruminated over the memory.

"Dutch oven, hell!" he said. "They left that camp *twenty-two* years before I found it."

In 1934 they buried Shorty Harris on the west side of the Valley, beside his old friend Jim Dayton who had died there in 1899.

The inscription on the double grave reads:

> *Bury Me Beside Jim Dayton in the Valley We Loved. Above Me Write: 'Here Lies Shorty Harris, a Single Blanket Jackass Prospector.' Epitaph Requested by Shorty (Frank) Harris, Beloved Gold Hunter. 1856–1934. Here Jas. Dayton, Pioneer, Perished, 1898.* To These Trail Makers Whose Courage Matched the Dangers of the Land, This Bit of Earth is Dedicated Forever.*

One who was present at that burial tells me the hole they made for Harris was a bit too small. Actually, Shorty was only five feet tall, but even so the gravediggers had skimped, not allowing a little extra space for the coffin.

It was hot work to hew out extra inches in the hard soil.

"Hell, let it be," an ancient friend of the deceased advised. "Just take him out and *bend* him a little. Shorty won't mind."

---

* The inscription is incorrect by one year.

Apparently as a labor-saving device they did put the coffin in the ground at an angle, head up. That would have pleased Shorty, just as it was nice to know you were buried in what must be the *deepest* grave in America, this one being so considerably below sea level.

Shorty Harris, whose official name was Frank, was born in Rhode Island in 1856 or 1857. Twenty years later he came to California with Ulysses S. Grant. The general, on a speaking tour, rode in his private car, and Shorty rode the rods. Thereafter the saloons of Tombstone, Virginia City, Bodie, Silver Peak, and intermediate points knew him. On St. Patrick's Day of 1892 his golden odyssey really began when he and John Lambert struck it rich in the Panamint Mountains. Shorty liked to find gold, but not to mine it. One discovery after another he sold out promptly, and promptly spent what he got. The details of business bored him. Or frightened him. For apparently Shorty could neither read nor write.

The St. Patrick mine brought seven thousand dollars. Later Shorty found copper near what became Greenwater, which did him no good because his partner got drunk and forgot to file the claims. Then in 1904 he located the Bullfrog Mine which launched Rhyolite, and later had a hand in the discoveries at Harrisburg and Skidoo. Toward the end, when his luck with gold seemed to run out, "the Short Man," as he called himself, fell back on being a sort of oracle of the desert. His day—and the era of the like of him—was past, but in that day Shorty was the country's most colorful character among all the practicing prospectors.

He worked at being a character, too, a worthy runner-up to Death Valley Scotty. He covered less territory, but he had less to work with. Shorty got his gold from the mines, the hard way.

Jim Dayton, whom Shorty Harris chose to join in the eternity of Death Valley, was caretaker at the old Furnace Creek Ranch for fifteen years. Then, in the winter of 1898, he brought back a bride from Los Angeles who endured life well enough through the cool winter and the flowery spring. But when summer came she persuaded Jim he just had to return her to Los Angeles, which he did. Soon afterward he resigned his ranch job and prepared to follow her. He sent an Indian ahead, over the mountains to Ballarat, with a letter saying he was coming. When his letter reached his friends it was a long time overdue, because his postman liquored up at Ballarat. They were worried and Frank Tilton set out to see what was wrong.

That was midsummer, and a hard trip for Tilton and Dolph Navares who went with him.

In the dancing heat of the desert they found Jim Dayton's wagon, its four horses dead in their traces, and behind it the bodies of the two led horses, their heads held up to the end-gate by their short halters.

The reins of the horses in front had been slashed through to let them find their way to water and perhaps life, *but the brake had been set.* In that final effort to free his animals, the old twenty-mule swamper had forgotten to release the brake. Unable to move the wagon, the horses had perished. With his dog barking beside it, they found Jim's body near a clump of mesquite. He had died there, probably taken quickly by some sudden illness.

Frank Tilton says it wasn't much of a funeral. Thinking back over forty years, his memory of what he said is this: "Well, Jimmie, you lived in the heat and you died in the heat, and after what you been through I guess you ought to be comfortable in hell."

About death in Death Valley there was no solemnity. *Re-*

quiescat in pace, the desert man who set out to change his way of life, the single blanket jackass prospector.

It would be hard to find many aspects of Death Valley living or dying that are not adorned by some tale involving Scotty. About graves there is a special and macabre one.

In 1909 three Los Angeles acquaintances of Scotty decided that they wanted to see for themselves the mine he was supposed to have. Scotty, though ostensibly leading them mineward, took care that they never saw it. Sidney Norman, then editor of the *Los Angeles Mining Review,* one of the disillusioned trio, recorded what happened in a nettlesome little booklet he called, *Chasing Rainbows in Death Valley.* From start to finish everything about the trip was contrived to discourage the investigators, and discouraged they ultimately were, like everyone else who ever tried to find Scotty's mythical mine.

On the third day out they camped at Hidden Springs, where Scotty casually pointed out two graves of men he said had been murdered. Norman writes that the next morning he examined the graves. They were phony. The ground beneath the window dressing of piled up rocks had not been moved.

At least those, in all the roster of Death Valley's dead, were dummies, contrived from Scotty's peculiar imagination.

4. The Emigrants

*T*HE white man's history of Death Valley began in the winter of 1849–50.

Like so much else of the second chapter of California's story —following the Spanish era which was golden in a different way—the Valley's discovery stemmed from the fever that started near Sutter's Fort on January 28, 1848. That was the day James Marshall found flakes of gold and nuggets in the water race of the lumber mill the Swiss emigrant, John A. Sutter, was building.

The fever spread from the banks of the Sacramento out across the Mother Lode country, and across all America.

In December of '49, about a hundred emigrants came upon Death Valley in their scramble toward El Dorado. Until then no explorer, including the ubiquitous John Charles Frémont, had been closer than a hundred miles to the south.

The story of that journey of accidental discovery really starts in Utah Territory.

It was late in that autumn of '49 that the travelers trailed in from the east to the country about Salt Lake, with their covered wagons, their oxen, horses, women, children, and high hopes. The Mormons warned them winter was too close to risk the direct route across the Sierra through what is now the state of Nevada. Only three years before, the Donner Party, caught by the snows, had met tragedy that way.

How, then, to reach California? And quickly. For obviously it was folly to lose any time in getting to the gold fields where everyone would become so rich so soon.

Captain Jefferson Hunt, formerly of the Mormon "California Battalion," had traveled the Old Spanish Trail to the Mojave River and by way of Cajon Pass on to the Pueblo de Los Angeles. To be sure, wagons had not gone that way before, but packtrains had and doubtless with patience and luck wagons could. Anyway, for a fee of ten dollars for each wagon Hunt would guide the travelers on this circuitous route to the gold fields, and shortly around a hundred wagons started from near Provo, Utah, under his direction.

These travelers were typical of the times. Theirs was the same pioneer strain that earlier had peopled the valleys of the Cumberland and the plains of Indiana and Iowa. They were a part of the great section of America that was on the move, the magnets of good land and tall timber drawing the unanchored westward long before California gold quickened the tempo.

For the first days life went well with the wagon train. The women had their Bibles, the men their banjos. Despite discomfort and hard work, there were contentment and fine dreams of golden tomorrows. And in the evening, beside the campfires, singing.

> *We've formed our band, we are all well manned,*
> *To journey afar to the promised land;*
> *The golden ore is rich in store*

25

On the banks of the Sacramento shore.
Then ho, boys, ho! For California, O!
There's plenty of gold, so I've been told,
On the banks of the Sacramento!

Then the fires commenced to lose their cheerfulness. There was less to burn, as the country became more barren, only sagebrush and greasewood. Less feed for the oxen, too. And budding doubts for the wayfarers.

Perhaps Hunt knew less of the long trail than he thought he knew. Because of some minor misjudgments during the very first weeks, confidence in his leadership waned. And in that situation along came "Captain" O.K. Smith with a "map" he said he had from an old trapper named Barney Wood. This document, Smith declared, showed a route to California quicker, easier, shorter than the roundabout one Hunt proposed to follow. Roughly, it led westerly over mountains no one of them knew anything about, to Owens Lake and thence pretty directly to the gold fields beyond Walker Pass across the Sierra.

Just before the schism over the two trails became final—the one reasonably well traveled and long, the other unknown and shorter—William Lewis Manly came upon the scene. His own book, *Death Valley in '49*, is the odyssey of his long trek from St. Albans, Vermont, to California. Though written almost forty years later the account is remarkable for its clarity, precise detail, and good sense. So far as I know no other authentic journal of an emigrant who was neither professional explorer nor man of letters, equals it. The first chapters deal with the earlier stages of the lad's carefree journey from New England across all of America, by buggy, wagon, boat, horseback, and afoot. It was not all in one continuous stretch, of course, and it started when Lewis was only ten years old.

Manly came upon the wagon train some sixty miles south of Salt Lake. Eight days before that meeting, young Lewis (he was twenty-nine) and John Rogers, who figured gallantly with him in later events, had given up a hazardous attempt to navigate the Colorado River—of whose dangers they knew nothing—and had struck off along dubious Indian Trails to find the Mormon settlements.

All the long way from Wisconsin, which lay immediately behind him, Manly had hoped to catch up with friends, the Asahel Bennetts. He had lived with them at Mineral Point, and to them, when they started out ahead, he had entrusted his small belongings because they were traveling by wagon and he afoot. But even at the crossing of the rivers, where emigrants were wont to leave news of themselves, Manly had missed his friends. What was his joyful amazement, then, to discover that by some miracle they were in this wagon train he had overtaken by mere chance.

The Bennetts were as glad to see Manly as he them. "John Rogers," he noted, "had a dollar and a half and I had thirty dollars," which was no princely reserve to be stranded with in Utah in those, or any days.

Of the morning after the meeting, Manly wrote: "After breakfast Mr. Bennett said to me: 'Now Lewis, I want you to go with me; I have two wagons and two drivers and four yoke of good oxen and plenty of provisions. I have your outfit yet, your gun and ammunition and your two good hickory shirts. You need not do any work. You just look around and kill what you can.'"

With his hickory shirts and his precious rifle Manly became the hunter, guide, and ultimately the historian of the expedition; and later when his friends all but perished in Death Valley he it was who saved them.

In his book Manly describes the crisis when the adherents

of Smith and his map broke away from the followers of Hunt who kept to their planned course:

It was really a serious moment when the front of the train reached the Smith Trail. Team after team turned to the right while now and then one would keep straight ahead as was first intended. Captain Hunt came over to the larger party after the division was made and wished them all a hearty farewell and a pleasant, happy journey. My friend Bennett, whose fortune I shared, was among the seceders who followed the Smith party. This point where our paths diverged was very near the place afterward made notorious as Mountain Meadows, where the famous massacre took place (four years later) under the direction of the Mormon generals.

From the very start all of them were lost, so far as any fixed route was concerned. The beguiling map was a fraud, and Manly who really knew nothing of it, knew as much of the country as anyone, map or no map, and emerged as their best pathfinder.

As I had no team to drive I took every opportunity to climb the mountains along the route, reaching the highest elevations even if they were several miles from the trail. I sometimes remained out all night. I took Mr. Arcane's field glasses with me and was thus able to see all there was of the country. I soon became satisfied that going north was not taking us in the direction we ought to go. I frequently told them so, but they still persisted in following on. I went to the leaders and told them we were going back toward Salt Lake again, not making any headway toward California. . . . I told them, and Mr. Bennett and others, that we must either turn west, or retrace our steps and get back into the regular Los Angeles road again. In the morning we held another consultation and decided to turn west here, and leave the track we had been following.

Progress was by trial and error, and knowledge came the hard way. "We had to learn how to look for water in those

28

peculiar conditions. In my Wisconsin travel I had learned that when I struck a ravine I must go down to look for living water, but here we must invariably travel upward, for the water was found only in the high mountains."

Knowing what we know today, it is easy to wonder how anyone could have been so unwise as to undertake what these men did. The answer, of course, is that they had no idea of what they were getting into. Each time they saw high mountains to the west they thought them to be the Sierras, although actually several other ranges intervened.

Westing was what they wanted. The lure of gold and the bliss of ignorance propelled them. Only the *shortest* way to the goal was worth trying. Shortest in miles, but nothing else. For in that region the high mountains flow from the north to the south, where they finally smooth out into broad passes leading easily toward the Pacific. Even after reaching Death Valley, instead of following the natural way that led around by the south, the poor people scaled the mountain walls that stretched squarely across their path. They scrambled over not one, but three such ranges, like furrows in a ploughed field, each of them a mile and more high, each trailless and uncharted, each bare and baked and treeless.

The stubborn ones who kept on—various wagons turned back from time to time to rejoin Hunt on the Spanish Trail —became divided into several groups. The Jayhawkers, thirty young men from Illinois with twenty wagons, was one party. Then there were the Georgians, the Mississippi Boys, the Brier family, and the Manly-Bennett party. Later the Wade party left the Bennetts and struck out for itself, after Death Valley had been reached.

Of course, there were not at all times exact distinctions and separations between one party and another. Nor are the records at all complete or clear. For instance, the exhaustive

29

research made by Carl I. Wheat has disclosed the names (some of them incomplete) of only seventy of the approximate one hundred who came to Death Valley that winter, and that list included the three Negro slaves, Tom, Joe, and "Little West," who were with the Mississippi Boys.

Even the spelling of the principal characters' names is sometimes dubious. For instance, Wheat, who traced him quite literally from the cradle to the grave, has Bennett's first name as Asahel; yet Manly wrote it "Asabel," with which Edwin Corle's recent book, *Desert Country*, concurs, while the Federal Writers Project Guide offers "Asa."

An entire volume could be written about what is known and surmised of the adventures of these emigrants from the time they left Hunt in Utah until they straggled into the California settlements. Here it seems appropriate to touch only on the highlights. If you are interested in following the known and somewhat involved details of that period, by all means read the scholarly publication by Carl Wheat entitled, *Trailing the Forty-Niners Through Death Valley*. In this, and other papers, Mr. Wheat has done a magnificent historical job.

Of the wagons which on November fourth turned from Hunt to take the "short-cut" route, twenty-seven were still rolling on Christmas Day, 1849, when all had reached a point well within what is now Death Valley National Monument.

Since then probably there has been no Christmas as dismal on Furnace Creek, for that is where they camped, probably within a few miles of the site of the present inn. A short hundred years ago that could be a most unpleasant place. Manly writes:

During my absence from camp for two days, the Indians had shot arrows into three of our oxen, and one still had an arrow in his side forward of the hip, which was a dangerous place. To
30

be sure and save him for ourselves we killed him. Some were a little afraid to eat the meat, thinking perhaps the arrow might be poisoned, but I argued that they wanted meat themselves and would not do that. I told them if they got a shot themselves it would very likely be a poisoned arrow and they must take the most instant measures to cut it out before it went into the blood. So we ventured to dry the meat and take it with us. . . . We pulled the arrows out of the other oxen and they seemed to sustain no great injury from the wounds.

From the camp beside this "little faint stream" the Bennetts and the Arcanes decided "it was evidently the best way to turn south and make our own road, and find the water and passes all for ourselves," rather than trail along behind the Jayhawkers, as they had been doing. The Jayhawkers struck northwestward across the Valley while Manly's party "rolled down the canyon [Furnace Creek] and out into the valley and then turned due south."

Soon they saw that they must cross to the western side because the way along the foot of the eastern walls—probably about where the road now runs toward Badwater—was too rough with caked salt, where it leveled out below the impassible rocky going, for the oxen to navigate. That meant crossing the salt flats, then just about as they are today, some of them covered with water.

"I got a mesquite stick with which to sound out our way, rolled up my pants, pulled off my moccasins and waded in." So began this first traverse of Death Valley in its very midregions, and at a place perhaps two hundred feet below sea level, though the pioneers knew nothing of that. Continued Manly:

Striking my stick on the bottom, it seemed solid rock, and breaking off a small projecting point I found it to be solid rock salt. As the teams rolled along they scarcely roiled the water. It looked

31

to me as if the whole valley, which might be a hundred miles long, might have been a solid bed of rock salt. Before we reached this water there were many solid blocks of salt lying around covered with a little dirt on the top.

Near a century later, other sorts of explorers found how solid indeed was that "bed of rock salt," when drilling showed its depth to be 1800 feet!

The second night we found a good spring of water coming out from the bottom of the snow peak almost over our heads. This was a temporary relief, but it brought us face to face with stranger difficulties and a more hopeless outlook.

There was no possible way to cross this high steep range of mountains anywhere to the north. The Jayhawkers had abandoned their wagons and burned them, and we could no longer follow the trail they made. It seemed that there was no other alternative but for us to keep along the edge of the mountain to the south and search for another pass. Some who read Fremont's travels said that the range immediately west of us must be the one he described, on the west side of which was a beautiful country, of rich soil and having plenty of cattle and horses, and containing some settlers, but on the east all was barren, dry, rocky sandy desert as far as could be seen. We knew this eastern side answered well the description and believed that this was really the range described, or at least it was close by.

Again, they thought this barrier range was the Sierra. The will-o'-the-wisp of golden California lay just beyond! Only, of course, in truth it did not. This "snow peak almost over our heads" was Telescope, and the mountains the Panamints. Beyond them lay another range before the Sierra even came in view, except from the summits themselves.

Today it is so easy to see what these people should have done. That's a prime virtue of retrospection. The courage of what they did is no less than the misfortune of their choice.

32

At least, what Manly wrote of this trial-and-error exploring helps one to understand the reasoning that at the moment seemed sound.

We had to look over the matter very carefully and consider all the conditions and circumstances of the case. We could see the mountains were lower to the south, but they held no snow and seemed only barren rocks piled up in lofty peaks, and as we looked it seemed the most Godforsaken country in the world.

We had been in the region long enough to know the higher mountains contained most water, and that the valleys had bad water or none at all, so that while the lower altitude to the south gave some promise of easier crossing it gave us no promise of water or grass, without which we must certainly perish.

So it looked to Manly, a brave, competent, strong young man confronted with problems for which the experience of none of them held any precedents.

Meantime, while they camped there to the west of the salt in the shadow of the Panamints—the place was either Bennett's Wells or Tule Springs—some of the teamsters left them and went to join the Jayhawker party which already was trudging northward, their wagons burned and the dried meat of their oxen on their backs, around the bulwarks of the Panamints and ultimately through what came to be called Jayhawker Canyon, close to where the Lone Pine Road now traverses Towne's Pass.

While to the north the Jayhawkers and the others were fighting for survival, and the Bennett-Arcane party loitered miserably at the springs, upon one little group alone among all those unhappy people good fortune laid its hand. At dawn, following a disconsolate night discussion of what best to do, without a word to anyone else the Wade family spanned their oxen and drove away. There was Henry Wade, born in England and just turned fifty years; his wife Mary, from London; and Harry, Charles, Almira, and Richard, their ages fourteen, eleven, nine, and five.

They turned neither to the mountains, where water should be, nor northward where the others went, but south by way of the dry bed of the Amargosa to Saratoga Springs, a natural oasis at the lower end of Death Valley, and then by way of the jack-in-the-box Mojave River to Cajon Pass and safety. A desperate journey which we soft-livers of today scarcely could hope to survive. But the Wades did it, bringing through their oxen, and their children safe and sound, and one wagon or two, the number being uncertain, though the fact is sure that no other survived of the thirty-seven wagons which rolled westward from that tragic division point in Utah.

Before the Wades left, there had been a meeting, a forum of survival. Life and Death were its agenda. Everyone who wished had his say.

"One thing was certain: we must move somewhere at once." Manly's memory of that fact is sure.

If we stayed here we could live as long as the oxen did, and no longer, and if we went on it was uncertain where to go to get a better place. We had guns and ammunition, to be sure, but of late we had seen no living creature in this desert wild. Finally, Mr. Bennett spoke and said:

"Now I will make you a proposition. I propose that we select two of our youngest, strongest men and ask them to take some food and go ahead on foot to try to seek a settlement, and food, and we will go back to the good spring we have just left and wait for their return. It will surely not take them more than ten days for the trip, and when they get back we shall know all about the road and its character and how long it will take us to travel it. They can secure some other kind of food that will make us feel better, and when the oxen have rested a little at the spring we

34

can get out with our wagons and animals and be safe. I think this is the best and safest way. Now what do you all say?"

After a little discussion all seemed to agree that this was the best, and now it remained to find the men to go. No one offered to accept the position of advance messengers. Finally Mr. Bennett said he knew one man well enough to know that he would come back if he lived, and he was sure he would push his way through. "I will take Lewis (myself) if he will consent to go." I consented, though I knew it was a hazardous journey. We would be exposed to all sorts of things—Indians, climate, and probably lack of water—but I thought I could do it and would not refuse. John Rogers, a large strong Tennessee man, was then chosen as the other one and he consented also.

Now preparations began. Mr. Arcane killed the ox which had so nearly failed, and all the men went to drying and preparing meat. Others made us some new moccasins out of rawhide, and the women made us each a knapsack.

Our meat was closely packed, and one can form an idea how poor our cattle were from the fact that John and I actually packed seven-eighths of all the flesh of an ox into our knapsacks and carried it away. They put in a couple of spoonfuls of rice and about as much tea. This seemed like robbery to the children, but the good women said that in case of sickness even that little bit might save our lives. I wore no coat or vest, but took half of a light blanket. We each had a small tin cup and a small camp kettle holding a quart. Bennett had me take his seven-shooter rifle, and Rogers had a good double barreled shot gun. We each had a sheath knife, and our hats were small brimmed, drab affairs fitting close to the head, which would not be very conspicuous to an enemy if we should rise up from behind a hill into possible views. We tried on our packs and fitted the straps a little so they would carry easy. They collected all the money there was in camp and gave it to us. Mr. Arcane had about thirty dollars and the others threw in small amounts from forty cents upward.

35

So young Manly and John Rogers set out. Left in the camp were the Bennetts and their children, George, Melissa, and and Martha; J. B. Arcane, his wife and infant son, Charles, and others including Captain Culverwell—"a sea-faring man"— and the Earhart brothers, in all eleven adults beside the Wade family.

The relief expedition was expected back in ten days. Twenty-six days passed before it returned. By then, sunk in discouragement and the fear that they had been deserted, all but the Bennetts and Arcanes had left that lonely camp to try their individual fortunes. And Culverwell was dead.

That Good Samaritan journey of Manly and Rogers is an epic in itself, set within the pattern of the overall odyssey. Some ninety other members of the party each had his individual adventures, many no doubt affecting, had we record of them. But of all those first wayfarers in Death Valley, the only account that survives is Manly's. If you would have its graphic details read for yourself his book.°

Emaciated, exhausted, lame, starved, and thirsting, finally they came to the Green Pastures. The trees, the grass, the water, and the good food that waited, seemed far finer than any gold could be.

How they contrived to conquer the two hundred and fifty miles of trackless mountains and searing deserts is a miracle. But conquer them they did, and the memory of that journey's end in the first days of the year 1850—the exact date is uncertain—remained vivid in Manly's mind when he wrote of it forty years later.

The summit of the last low mountains beyond the Mojave Desert reached,

---

° *Death Valley in '49.* Written about 1888, published first in 1894 at San Jose, California, and republished in 1929 and again in 1946 by Wallace J. Hebberd, Santa Barbara, California.

a most pleasing sight filled our sick hearts with a most indescribable joy. I shall never have the ability to describe adequately the beauty of the scene as it appeared to us, and so long as I live that landscape will be impressed upon my memory as the most cheering in the world. There before us was a beautiful meadow of a thousand acres, green as a thick carpet of grass could make it, and shaded with oaks, wide branching and symmetrical, equal to those of an old English park; while all over the low mountains that bordered it on the south and over the broad acres of luxuriant grass was a herd of cattle numbering many hundreds, if not thousands. They were of all colors and sizes. . . . Such a scene of abundance and rich plenty and comfort bursting thus upon our eyes, which for months had seen only the desolation and sadness of the desert, was like getting a glimpse of Paradise.

But having glimpsed that paradise, they resolutely turned from it as quickly as they could, to go back again all those long desert miles with the aid that meant life for the parents and four children who waited. The conscience of some could have been stilled by whispering that there was no use in returning because by that time all who had not escaped to safety surely would be dead. Which indeed was a likely enough assumption.

But Manly and Rogers went back. They took with them two horses and a little one-eyed mule and all the supplies they could carry. These horses were the final sacrifice. On the scramble across the Panamints they came to a dry water-fall the poor animals could not clamber over, though with stones set up in a sort of ramp the mule could. So there the horses were left to perish.

On that mountain trail they found the grave of the man named Isham, and the unburied body of Fish near the crest of the divide, both Jayhawkers who had died seeking escape to the west.

Then, on the twenty-sixth day from the time they had left the Valley of Despondency, they were there again. As they moved down the slopes toward the site of the camp, Manly, who had delayed to fix his moccasins, came up to Rogers leaning on his gun and waiting.

"Here is Captain Culverwell. Dead." Rogers' words were ominous. What other bodies might they find?

About noon they came in sight of the wagons, grouped in a small depression. When they left, there had been seven wagons. Now there were only *four,* and they seemed dismantled, the covers stripped from them.

One can imagine the misgivings of the two young men as they approached. Now only a hundred yards away, they saw no signs of life at all.

It was Manly who fired his Colt rifle, for he had seven charges left, while Rogers had but two.

The shot sounded strangely loud in the vast silence of the desert, but for a space not a move could they see.

Then, "as if by magic," as Manly remembers, a man came out from under a wagon.

They were there, all of them, the Bennetts and the Arcanes, scarecrows but alive. Despite the tragedy of their surroundings no reunion could have been more joyful than that one beside the salt flats as the afternoon shadows of the Panamints marched purple across the gleaming waste. Never since has the Valley encompassed deeper thanksgiving.

No doubt the event of that heartfelt reunion that meant most to little Charlie Arcane and Martha Bennett and her older sister and brother, were the surprising yellow balls "Uncle Lewis" brought them. Never before had these youngsters from Illinois and Wisconsin seen the like, or tasted such juicy sweetness once the odd wrinkled skin was peeled. A

Mexican woman at the faraway, fairy-story rancho had sent them for the children—four California oranges.

After they had eaten and rested, with the children slung on the backs of the scrawny oxen in makeshift pack-saddles contrived from the canvas wagon covers, they made their way to the settlements, ultimately reaching San Francisquito Rancho in Newall on March 7, 1850.

The story has an incredible aftermath. Ten years from this very time Manly was again in Death Valley with Bennett, whose life he had saved. This time the situation was exactly reversed. It was Manly who was left on the desert, caring for a sick companion, Charles Alvord, while Bennett with a man named Twitchell went for help. *They never came back.* If Manly had not been found by the George party he and Alvord would have perished. Manly never saw Bennett again, but years afterward he encountered Twitchell who told him that Bennett and he had been held up for six weeks by a storm and decided it was then too late to save the men they had abandoned. Manly wrote, thirty-five years later, "It required some grace to become reconciled to this yarn."

5. White Gold

THAT chronicle of the gold-seekers of 1849–50 is the essence of Death Valley's story. The next thirty years did not contribute much literary paydirt for the historian. Compared to the concentrated drama of those first months the events that followed have been diluted by elapsed time, though mixed with humor, too, and rich with the zest of variety.

Two physicians, Doctors E. Darwin French and S. A. George, headed separate expeditions to the Valley in 1860, first proponents of that famous outdoor sport of the desert, looking for lost mines, the same being a Western replica of that old New England custom of searching for buried treasure. The Gunsight * was one such lost mine, a will-o'-the-wisp of silver, and another bore the name of Jacob Breyfogle, a blacksmith of Austin, Nevada, who prospected in 1864 and came back with rock samples rich in gold and a mind so affected by the sun he could not remember where he found them. Natu-

* See Chapter entitled "Panamint Valley."

40

rally, optimists, with all sorts of plausible hunches and secret information, have been tracking the Breyfogle ever since.

In the year 1861 Death Valley saw some surveying and several camels * and in 1870 a sizable military expedition made reports on the country which, with official un-wisdom, they chose to visit in the summer when survival was about the most one could reasonably hope to accomplish. In 1875 Lieutenant Rogers Birnie, jr., did a better job, and increasingly, as access became easier, the Valley became better known.

Following that period of discovery, the Valley's solid history is moved forward not by gold or silver, but by a far more prosaic product.

"She burns green, Rosie! We're rich!"

In the bright lexicon of Death Valley's literature, that phrase ranks right along with welkin-ringers like "Lafayette, we are here," and "Don't give up the ship." And in its environment, it is quite as deathless.

As with the exact christening of the Valley itself, there is uncertainty as to just who set down Aaron Winter's historic exclamation. Either Aaron became his own chronicler—one can imagine him trying out phrases to find the one that would sound best to posterity—or Rosie herself recorded it.

Anyway, with those or other appropriate words, uttered in a poverty-stricken cabin in Ash Meadows about 1880, Death Valley's fortune was launched. For borax was discovered, and borax made the Valley what it is today in the human scheme of things.

Despite the millions of dollars paid in for mining stocks, and the lesser millions extracted from the mines, the fact remains that gold, silver, lead, and copper, with temporary

* See Chapter 16, "Amargosa Country."

exceptions, did not at all balance their several books throughout this region of geological chaos. Which held true from
the tough boom of Panamint City to the more refined swin-
dlings later at Leadfield.

But borax has paid its way. And apparently always will, for
the supply seems almost inexhaustible.

No one ever did anything about preserving Aaron Winter's
home where Death Valley borax was born. I suppose, in its
way, that historic landmark compares with that law office in
Springfield, Illinois, or Edison's first laboratory. But at least
Mr. C. M. Plumb set down such a faithful picture of that sad
little home—and a very great many desert shacks are not so
different today—that to read it is to understand better what
sudden fortune meant to Rosie and her husband.

Close against the hill, one side half-hewn out of the rock, stood
a low stone building, with a tule-thatched roof. The single room
within was about fifteen feet square. In front was a canvas-
covered addition of about the same size. The earth, somewhat
cleared of broken rock originally there, served as a floor for
both rooms. There was a door to the stone structure, and directly opposite this was a fire-place, while a cook-stove stood on
a projecting rock at one side of it. At the right was a bed, and
at the foot of the bed a few shelves for dishes. A cotton curtain
was stretched over some clothing hanging on wooden pegs in
the corner.

On the other side was the lady's boudoir—a curiosity in its
way. There was a window with a deep ledge there. A newspaper
with a towel covered the ledge, in the center of which was a
starch box supporting a small looking-glass. On each side of the
mirror hung old brushes, badly worn bits of ribbon and some
other fixings for the hair. Handy by was a lamp-mat lying on
another box, and covered with bottles of Hogan's Magnolia
Balm, Felton's Gossamer for the Complexion, and Florida Water
—all, alas, empty, but still cherished by the wife, a comely, deli-

cate Spanish-American woman with frail health and little fitted for the privations of the desert.

These shelves about the room and the rude mantel over the fire-place were spread with covers made of notched sheets of newspaper. Two rocking chairs had little tidies on their backs. The low flat pillows were covered with pillow shams and the bed itself with a tawny spread. In place of a library there were a number of copies of the Police Gazette. There was a flour barrel against the wall, a small bag of rice near by, and two or three sacks of horse feed in a corner. The sugar, coffee and tea were kept under the bed.

The water of the spring ran down the hill and formed a pool in front of the house, and here a number of ducks and chickens, with a pig and a big dog formed a happy group, a group that rambled about in the house as well as romped beside the water of the spring. A few cattle grazed on the bunch-grass of the valley that stretched away before the house, gray and desolate.

It was just two hundred miles across the desert from this home to the nearest settlement or railroad station.

Aaron Winter's saga started some days before the Great Discovery when a nameless prospector stopped for the night at the shack on Ash Meadows where the bottles of Florida Water were empty. That visitor told his host of borax and its value—in those days fifty cents a pound as a drug—described the marshes where it was found, and explained a simple test producing a green flame that identified the precious stuff.

As soon as they could, Winter, his wife, and his pack burros set out for Death Valley. There, beyond Furnace Creek Wash, were the formations he was thinking of as the prospector had talked and he had asked questions. The pack-saddles they filled with the white woolly stuff crushed from the "cotton-balls" that look the same today as they did then, and once home at Ash Meadows and with darkness around them, Aaron prepared the chemicals as he had been told.

On the white salts in a saucer Aaron poured the solution.
He lit a match. The flame caught. It burned green.

"She burns green, Rosie. We're rich, by God!"

That is the story historians are stuck with. It has rolled
along since 1880, though no one has told just where the chemicals came from that Aaron used. Perhaps the overnight guest
had them along and graciously left them.

In 1881 Winter sold his borax claims to W. T. Coleman for
twenty thousand dollars and for an additional five thousand
dollars the water rights to Texas Springs. Perhaps Rosie
would have preferred moving somewhat nearer the sources
of Florida Water and other feminine niceties, but they ended
up on a goodly cattle ranch that Aaron bought in the Pahrump Valley.

Because no Columbus should be abandoned after his first
discovery, and since the human sequences of history are more
entertaining than the economic, we'll digress again to follow
Mr. Winter's story one page further.

On that cattle ranch at Pahrump two men, Parks and Ellis,
came one day to Aaron Winter, bringing some soapy white
stuff they'd found at the southern end of the Amargosa Valley.
Winter, of course, was something of a borax oracle by then.
Once more he did his magic with sulphuric acid and alcohol,
and again "it burned green." Parks and Ellis and Winter each
got five thousand from Coleman, who forthwith established
the Amargosa Borax Works, a convenient place to absorb his
idle labor during the summer shut-downs in Death Valley.

With this new windfall, Winter went to Belmont, county
seat of Nye County, to pay his taxes and have a little fun. As
a contribution to humor he placed a broken six-gun on top
of twelve hundred dollars in the jockey box of his wagon. Before he got to Belmont he put in a night, and considerable

drinks, with two fellow guests at a stage station. The next morning the station-tender's wife mentioned that the other two men were just leaving and did Winter happen to have anything valuable in that jockey box because she had seen them poking in it?

Investigation showed the twelve hundred dollars and the broken gun were gone. But Winter's fellow guests had not. One immediately covered him with the stolen gun and told him to run along about his business. Instead of which Aaron drew his own good gun and killed the fellow, in whose pockets he found the twelve hundred dollars. Winter and the other man loaded the corpse in the wagon and proceeded to Belmont where quick trial was had and the whole matter tidied up. At the end of it Aaron hired the dead robber's companion as a ranch hand.

There may be several morals to this true tale. Likely one of them is that the criminally inclined should never point a pistol that won't shoot at a man who knows it won't shoot.

Now, back to borax.

About 1880 Isadore Daunet and three companions started the Eagle Borax Works—whose remains you still see, south of Bennett's Wells—but the low-grade product failed to bring enough to make the operation profitable and it was soon abandoned. Only one hundred and thirty tons of Eagle Borax were ever shipped.

Behind that prosaic story of a rainbow that panned out with no pot o' gold at its end, is another, reminiscent of Jim Dayton, who died on his way to rejoin his bride. After that first season of borax manufacture, when things looked not too bad, Daunet celebrated by marrying Clothilde Garraul. Winter or summer Mrs. Daunet would have none of Death Valley and the last time her husband returned to her in San Francisco she demanded a divorce. Daunet saved her the trouble by jumping out a window. Death Valley and married bliss seem to mix poorly.

Coleman, who bought from Winter, started the Harmony Borax Works in 1882. That was the same William T. Coleman who was born in the village of Cynthiana, Kentucky, by the oddest freak of circumstance the identical place whence came another character famous in the history of those deserts, Death Valley Scotty. The Harmony Works, which Coleman launched, you may see today, five miles north of Furnace Creek Inn, beside that tumbled area of "chocolate sundae" hillocks. There was launched what became America's best-publicized unit of pioneer transportation.

Moving the borax from Death Valley to Mojave was the necessity which mothered the invention of the famous Twenty Mule Teams. Their trade-mark has invaded most kitchens in America. A few of the old wagons themselves you may still see at Furnace Creek Ranch, hitched one behind the other, those pioneer "trailers" so very different from the modern streamlined products that currently grace the Texas Springs Auto Camp, within rifle shot of the old Harmony Works.

J. S. W. Perry, who had graduated from office work to the job of plant superintendent at the Harmony, set himself to designing something commodious and rugged in wagons for heavy hauling and rough treatment. Each one held ten tons, and they were built by J. T. Delameter at Mojave, and built so well that in the five years of their use they never gave out.

Two wagons, linked together as a lead and a trailer, were drawn by teams of twelve to twenty mules, the wheeler pair being, as a rule, horses. The lead pair of one of these jingling strings was harnessed one hundred feet in front of the lead wagon. Profanity and a cotton jerk line, half an inch thick, that ran through a ring on one mule in each pair exercised

46

some measure of control over this motive power. If the driver wished the leaders to go to the left he jerked the line; when he wished the team to go to the right he gave a steady pull.

Each outfit was handled by two men, a driver and a swamper. The driver drove and the swamper did everything else. Because it was a trying existence, they quarreled. Plenty of battling enlivened the Twenty Mule Team route, and occasional homicides.

On the long haul to Mojave there were only three wells. Between them the longest gap without water was fifty miles, which is a long way when loaded wagons can be moved only sixteen miles a day. Stopping places were built at sixteen-mile intervals, the dry camps furnished with a five-hundred-gallon tank of water and with hay and barley, these being replenished as the outfits returned empty. A round trip took about thirty days and the whole operation closed down during the hottest summer months.

In 1887 importations of borax from abroad brought the price so low the Death Valley works closed down, although the Twenty Mule Team insignia carried on. Coleman's organization in 1889 was sold to the Pacific Coast Borax Company, headed by F. M. ("Borax") Smith. Around the turn of the century there was little activity in Death Valley, but large quantities of borax were mined at Borate, near Daggett.

The Lila C., near Death Valley Junction, operated from 1907 to 1914, when the narrow-gauge railroad to Ryan was completed. In the meantime Smith was forced to liquidate and Pacific Coast Borax took over all his borax holdings. Ryan operated from 1914 to 1928, when its production was moved to Boron, near Mojave, where great deposits had been located close to rail transportation.

Ryan, however, remains a feature of the Death Valley country. The mine and its community of buildings are intact,

47

transformed into a resort usually operated by P.C.B. for a few winter months. Included in its attractions is a ride on the baby-gauge railroad whose Tom Thumb cars carry you through tunnels of borax and along the mountain slopes, with the vast reaches of the desert spread out below, and far to the west, beyond Death Valley, the ultimate skyline of the Sierra.

Borax, as I've said, made Death Valley what it is today. To it is owed the magnificent Inn, and Furnace Creek Ranch as well, both of them operated on private land by the Pacific Coast Borax Company, and both removed from any authority of the National Park Service, as the latter is wont to emphasize.

The man who first ranched where the Ranch now is—it was called Greenland Ranch in early days—appears slightly incredible, even among the galaxy of the Valley's eccentric characters.

Teck Bennett was his name, no kin to Asahel Bennett of the '49 party. This first semi-permanent resident has gone down in history as Bellerin' Teck, because he seems to have made more noise than had been heard locally since the earthquakes quit and the foldings, faultings, and tiltings quieted, a few thousand centuries before Bellerin' arrived in 1870. Teck brought water in a ditch down from Furnace Creek, brought quail from "outside," and started ranching. He declared himself owner not only of the acres he cultivated, but of all Death Valley as well. And as he was the only person within earshot—although that meant a long way, his voice being what it was—no argument ensued.

Then along came a Mormon named Jackson. The stranger had two oxen and Teck had land that needed plowing. Almost at once Death Valley's first partnership was formed. It survived maybe a month. Having someone around to hear him may have spoiled Teck, who before that had been bellerin' only to the unresponsive spaces. The story goes that during a violent quarrel Bellerin' Teck ran his partner off at the business end of a shotgun. The displaced Mormon went so fast he forgot to take his oxen with him, so they became an added increment to the ranch. After a couple of years, existence on Furnace Creek seems to have become too placid to suit the Bennett temperament, and he and his voice and the oxen departed.

The Valley's next residents of any considerable persistence were the Lee family who appeared about 1875. The four brothers had rarefied names, Leander, Philander, Meander, and Salamander. Although the records are hazy, Edwin Corle declares, on what authority I know not, that all the Lees were talented. Leander was notably proficient in creating half-breed reproductions of his kind; Philander could outswear the best of the mule-skinners; Meander excelled at applied idleness; and Salamander never spoke. When the classic motion picture of those Death Valley days is made, the Marx Brothers have a vehicle waiting.

Other pungent characters followed in the wake of the Lees and Bellerin' Teck. A good many of them, past and present, you encounter in these pages, however briefly. A whole book, indeed, could be written about the men, and some women, who have peopled Death Valley in the hundred years of its history. Perhaps never has a more odd and entertaining caste embellished a stranger stage.

The sum-total of what was accomplished by their labors, their lawlessness, their courage, their devotion, their optimism is Death Valley today. Even their lying is characteristic of the place. It is a poor human who would let the fantasies that Nature has made facts, outdo what his imagination could create.

6. "It's Not the Humidity"

*T*HE most talked-about feature of Death Valley is its climate. Especially its heat.

Listening to those whose fortunes are bound up with the Valley you are apt to encounter divergent schools of thought about temperatures. Some feel the hotter it sounds the more alluring it is. Others hold that the torridness should be soft pedaled lest it frighten away the tourist geese who lay the golden eggs.

Climatic discussions are apt to boil down into a yes-and-no pattern. By and large you gather that the Valley is the hottest place this side of Hell, but at that thoroughly salubrious. Verity is weighed on delicate balances.

Whatever Nature contrives, and however the figures are rigged, you can't please everyone. In a recent January we talked with friends from Minnesota, Arthur Otis and his wife, just back from their first Death Valley visit. To them, the very name had meant sweltering heat.

"Would you believe it," they all but upbraided me, "overcoats were comfortable in the evening. We expected the heat
50

would make trouble with the tires, but the only trouble we had was keeping warm in the shade."

"Well, it's midwinter," I reminded them. "Disappointed?"

"Sort of!" Arthur grinned. "But pleasantly."

Also, the horrors of Death Valley didn't measure up to the billing. In their hazy acquaintance with local history they'd supposed dozens of pioneers perished in that first exploration of 1849. It was something of a shock when Naturalist Alberts' lecture at Furnace Creek Ranch disclosed only one fatality. I think the customers felt cheated.

Temperature statistics add up to just this: In summer Death Valley is America's hottest place; in winter one of its most pleasant.

My homeopathic prescription for the inquiring visitor is to present the actual figures. Curiously, this has never been done before. I found some "highs" and "lows," and a fine crop of scorching weather yarns, but no one had dug systematically into the weather-station records. So E. E. Ogston, Chief Ranger, who for some years has kept the official meteorological observations, generously did just that, providing me with the first detailed record of Death Valley's climate.

During July and August the peak of daylight temperatures is usually between 120° and 128°. The average maximum high for July through ten years was 123.7°. In summer, night temperatures rarely fall below 85°. December and January are the coolest months. Climatic conditions in February, March, and April approach perfection.

How hot it gets in the sun is uncertain. Once when the thermometer in the shaded box of the weather station showed a mere 116°, another instrument laid out on the sun-drenched sand reached 160° before the mercury ran out of glass. Obviously the summer sun is to be avoided.

The temperatures depend entirely upon the time of year

51

you encounter them. The range is all the way from a record cold of 19° to an all-time high, in the shade, of 134°. That figure almost touches the world's top temperature, a dubious distinction held by Azizia, Tripoli, with 136°.

It is probable that we could bring the pennant for heat home to America if the Weather Bureau would authorize a recording station at Badwater, America's lowest spot, some twenty-two miles from the present thermometers at Greenland Ranch and Cow Creek, as the stations at Furnace Creek Ranch and Park Headquarters are officially called. For the greenery and irrigation, with increased humidity around the Ranch, affect the heat appreciably, holding down temperatures possibly several degrees. At Badwater, with no works of man to temper it, the heat would be absolute, and likely, unique. Such a station at Badwater would be 279.6 feet below sea level, compared with –178 at Greenland and –133 at Cow Creek.

It is interesting to note that an increasing number of visitors come just to see for themselves *how hot it really is.*

There is no reason why you should not sample the Valley in the summer if you wish.* It is not "closed." The roads are as good then as at any time, and patrolled in case of accident. While the hotels are closed (excepting Scotty's Castle, at three thousand feet) water is available and there are emergency accommodations at both Furnace Creek Ranch and Stovepipe Wells, and cabins in Wildrose Canyon.

"How hot does it get in summer?"

Rangers say that is the question most often asked.

Here are some figures which provide an answer to the universal curiosity, for all months of the year:

The average maximum for ten years is 100.5°.

The average minimum for ten years is 52.5°.

* See Park Service suggestions for summer travel in Appendix.

For the six months commencing with May, the average maximum temperatures for ten years ending with 1945, was 115.8°.

For the same summer period, the average minimum was 66.2°.

With caution, and shade, even summer temperatures are bearable, because the atmosphere is so very dry. The humidity often approaches zero and seldom exceeds six. Its average for twenty-eight recorded months was exactly four, and in 1945 there were two days of absolute zero humidity. Those figures may mean more if you know that the normal relative humidity throughout the United States averages about *sixty*. Discomforts are infinitely less than those of comparable temperatures in humid regions. In Death Valley it's not the humidity, it's the heat. And you get used to the heat. Park Service workers who have summered often in the Valley say existence, once you're acclimated, becomes reasonably pleasant.

"The first five years are the hottest," Ranger Sam Houston paraphrases.

Fortunately for them, it was in cool December that the first white men blundered into Death Valley when in 1849 they sought a short-cut to the El Dorados of California's coast. Even so, their oxen and their horses died, and some of the humans, too, though not in the Valley itself.

It was not heat, but lack of water and feed for themselves and their stock that brought disaster to the straying gold-seekers. Those things plus bad judgment unhappily coupled with the hardihood and courage we like to regard as prime characteristics of our pioneers. Not the climate, but lack of knowledge and human error was their worst enemy.

While the Valley has no real dangers in winter, the summer heat is not to be trifled with. It slows down mental processes and distorts judgment, as well as producing definite physiological reactions. The heat engendered in the body by the sun is like the fever created by infection, and is sometimes accompanied by delirium. A heart weakened by violent pumping of the blood to the surface of the body, and further exhausted by panic-stricken activity, suddenly stops. The air is so dry that perspiration dries almost as soon as it forms, leaving a coating of salt on the skin as gritty as fine sand.

An effect of this persistent salty evaporation is to draw salt from the body, with resulting weakness. That's why visitors to the Valley in summertime are urged to use salt pills. One with each meal is a moderate dose. Usually the pills can be assimilated without discomfort when taken with food, though some people have difficulty with them if they are used by themselves.

Automobiles, unfortunately, can't counteract evaporation with doses of salt, and radiators have a habit of going dry; so travelers through the Valley should always carry extra water.

In Death Valley summers, the venerable gag about being able to fry eggs on the fender of a car pretty nearly comes true. It's a fact that you'll burn your hand if you touch metal parts of a car exposed to the sun.

Then there is that odd observation about flies in summer, characteristic of standard Death Valley lore. After July first, they say, flies don't fly. They crawl. That's because their wings get burned off in the sun. Come the cool autumn, when temperatures get down around a hundred, the wings grow on again.

The heat does things to fruit, too—as well as to stories.

At one of the entrances to the Monument a tourist bought some oranges. They were miserable specimens, tiny and shriveled.

"Yes, Ma'am, something very special," the native son explained. "Dehydrated. The newest thing in California fruit."

54

As the lady wanted to know more, he explained the oranges were grown nearby in the hottest part of the desert.

"It's so hot the water sometimes boils when we irrigate the grove," he assured her. "This fruit dehydrates right there on the trees. Instead of having all that waste pulp, the sweetness is concentrated. Cooked right in, you see? They don't weigh more than half what a regular fat orange would"—which was true—"that's because all the water is dried out of 'em. Soak 'em and they swell up wonderful. Natural dehydration, that's what it is."

He handed the purchaser her dozen oranges.

"Now you take 'em home and put 'em in water. Tepid water." He pocketed his dollar. "And see what happens."

Temperature, of course, is but one element of climate. The Valley's overall climate, like its heat, depends upon *when* you visit it. Twenty-five thousand years ago it was quite different from now.

In those prehistoric yesterdays the prevailing weather of this weird region possibly was not unlike that currently encountered in Louisiana. Then the barren wastes, some of them now resembling pictures of the moon, was a lush land of ferns and exotic growths.

Actually, Death Valley's climate, as with all regions near the western coast, results from weather manufactured far out over the Pacific, mostly to the northwest. But before that weather reaches inland locales like the Valley, it is conditioned by the intervening mountains.

The region's particularized brand of weather is the natural product of the local geography. It is completely surrounded by mountains of its own, east of the Sierras, so that such rain-bearing clouds as may surmount the initial barrier have other hurdles to cross. By the time they reach this sunken desert the moisture in them is wrung dry by cooling, condensation, and precipitation. The occasional local summer rains are formed of water from the neighboring highlands, and that which falls in winter usually comes in over the fairly low ranges from the southwest.

If the Sierra Nevada were not where they are, Death Valley doubtless would be blessed by a considerable rainfall, its history and its name would have been different—and this book would not have been written.

For a million million years Nature has been violent in and about Death Valley. At times she still is.

In this land of little rain, a four-inch precipitation is considered a rousing wet season. The Valley's official average for ten years is 2.4 inches. For comparison, New York averages 43, San Francisco 22, Chicago 32 inches.

However, a single cloudburst can let down several inches all in one "bust" and all in one very restricted area. Unless the rigid boundaries of the storm happen to include a weather station, not a drop of that cloudburst will find its way into the record. If the cloudburst does hit a weather station, however, the station itself more than likely will be carried a couple of miles down the nearest wash that may have been bone-dry for a hundred years.

While at Furnace Creek the sun blazes in a sky cloudless overhead, at Skidoo a dozen miles distant the heavens may open, depositing in half an hour a flood which would add several inches to the records if it could be measured. Actually, in the San Gabriel Mountains of California, 1.02 inches of rainfall was recorded in *one minute*, and a gauge once caught 2.47 inches in three minutes—more precipitation than occurs in an average entire year in Death Valley!

Statistics about summer rains in desert country are pretty sketchy, but it seems likely that the worst cycles of such storms

follow periods of heavy snow in the mountains with the resulting abundance of run-off water, so that the temporary dry-
country lakes are fuller and more frequent. Continued hot
sunshine draws such water to the clouds along with the rising
currents of heated air, extracting as well all moisture from
the atmosphere itself.

Sometimes this thermal sucking-up process takes the form
of waterspouts, when you can see the liquid actually being
pulled aloft in corkscrew columns, mushrooming at the top
into blue-black clouds while the tight, twisted bases riot across
the countryside like evil, dancing dervishes. At sea a spout,
though ominous enough, is at least all water. But the more
rare desert variety combine sand and gravel and sizable stones
all whirled upward with the water. Even frogs and tiny fish
have "rained" down upon dry desert.

In their appearance waterspouts are of the same pattern
as sand-spouts, which are no more than enlarged editions of
the little dust devils you see of a summer's day rollicking along
country roads when the air is hot and breezes active.

With or without waterspouts—and they are phenomena
of the summer months—when the sky becomes saturated it
wrings itself dry. An orderly consummation is a shower or
sizable rain. The disorderly manifestation is a cloudburst.

A cloudburst is like the breaking of a paper bag full of
water. Everything in the path of the furious flood it drops upon
the earth is washed away. Especially it devastates lands where
the slopes are steep and bare of growth to absorb and check
the rushing waters.

Desert storms are dangerous. Every hillside, canyon, alluvial
fan, and silted valley bear witness to their savage power. And
of them all—wind, snow, and rain—cloudbursts are the worst.
They are the exclamation points in the orderly editing of

erosion, which for aeons in this Death Valley country has been smoothing out the jumbled authorship of earthquakes.

Throughout the desert country more human history has to do with cloudbursts than with quakes. There was the road built into the mining camp at Panamint City. If you journey up through the steep labyrinth of Surprise Canyon today you'll glimpse the site, at least, of that first road. Only twenty-two days after Bart McGee blasted out the pioneer highway— christened on July Fourth with enthusiasm, considerable liquor, and the triumphal passage of a buggy—the rains came and the road went. Every trace of it vanished down the canyon when the rainbags burst, together with much of the town itself.

There have been travelers on the arid floor of Death Valley for whom drowning was a more imminent threat than thirst. And in sight of Furnace Creek Inn, too. A few summers ago the wash below the hotel became a torrent which gouged out a strip of desolation, including some store buildings that used to nestle beneath the main structure.

Just the same thing happened years before when Billy Killingly was camped on the sands close to where the Inn now stands. A flash flood, born in the wash to the eastward, rushed through the night. Billy, hearing the approaching roar, rolled from his blankets and lit out for high ground. Before he reached it the silty torrent was up to his waist. A very few hours later, exactly where the water had been, not a single drop was visible. It was all bone-dry desert again. There was only the waste left in the flood's wake with the boulders that it had rolled there steaming complacently in the morning sunshine, static again for a century or so until another such storm might roll them a few feet or a few miles farther, depending upon its ferocity.

Not, you understand, that the Death Valley traveler need worry unduly about such paradoxes as floods in the desert.

Indeed, there are summers with not a drop of rain. Only when the rare rains do come, they are to be regarded with a considerable measure of respect.

Another idiosyncrasy of deserts, but not peculiar to Death Valley, is sandstorms. In the Valley they occur any time of year, during the winter perhaps once a month, in summer oftener. Sometimes they last only four hours. Like the rains, the full fury of a sandstorm is apt to be localized, though the dust and grit it stirs up may cover a large area. The summer storms are far worse than those of winter.

But at that it would be wrong to get the impression that Death Valley has a desperate climate, aside from the hottest months. During the tourist season—say, from the end of October to the first of May—there are few climates in all the world more thoroughly delightful.

59

7. Geologic Yesterdays

EVERY feature of Death Valley—appearance, climate, minerals, wild life, flora—stems from its geological history. Those, and its human aspects, are subjects for other chapters. This one outlines the story of geologic yesterdays responsible for today.

It is an involved record. Competent authorities differ as to its gigantic details. A million years separate the estimates of several as to when certain events occurred. But a mere million years seems such an insignificant time-factor in the reckoning of a geologist, a layman may pass such controversies by.

The quietest place on the world's surface is a true desert. In the dry heat there is next to no movement of animals or birds, and away from oases not even the leaves of trees to rustle.

Of all American deserts, Death Valley is the most still, if there can be degrees in the meaning of a word that is absolute. Certainly the Valley, apart from its human habitations, is a void of silence.

It is this absence of customary sound which strikes the perceptive visitor quite as deeply as does the scenery.

As the weird chaos on every hand becomes familiar, you realize what stupendous cataclysms in ancient ages shook this land to pieces and put it together again, not once but many times, with fire and quake and fantastic upheaval. And left the job only part-way done so that here, as no place else, are exposed cross-sections of a *billion* years of the making of the world.

What supernal bedlam must have raged where now all is so still, and what sublime pyrotechnics where the deserts are so peaceful!

Despite its appearance of permanence, right now the region is undergoing change, although in orderly and unspectacular cycles compared to the past. Man's conception of time is so insignificant we have no measuring sticks with which to appraise this instability. What change we cannot see in a year, say, quite escapes our attention. But even trivial remaking of landscapes may require a hundred or a thousand years.

Little as we are apt to note it, a trough like Death Valley is constantly lowering, while the hills around it are rising. And at that, both processes are camouflaged because erosion compensates for each, filling lowlands with what is washed off high places.

White man's history for Death Valley commenced one hundred years ago. That was in 1849.

Geologic history had its start perhaps two billion years earlier. The first chapter was written with fire and molten rock back in the Archaeozoic Age, a billion years before the remotest forebears of man emerged from nothingness.

A fascination of Death Valley, even to the casual observer, is that specific souvenirs of each of the five great periods of geologic history are found one place or another throughout the Monument. Beginning with the first or so-called Archean

61

period, through the Algonkian, Paleozoic, Mesozoic, and Cenozoic, the handwriting of time has left its record, its alphabet the rocks of ages, each a symbol with meaning peculiarly its own.

Rocks are of two general types, sedimentary and igneous. Sedimentary rocks are those that were deposited in the first place by wind or water as sand or mud and then hardened into rocks later by the pressure of the materials deposited, in turn, above them. Igneous rocks are those formed from the molten magma of the earth's interior. If these molten rocks cool so quickly that they do not have time to form crystals they become volcanic glass or obsidian. If they cool more slowly and form small crystals they become basalt or some other common volcanic rock. If they cool very slowly and under pressure they form very large crystals and become granite, or granite-like in texture.

The very old rocks in Death Valley were formed by these various means and were deposited to a very great thickness. After they had been deposited there was a long period, perhaps several million years, during which erosion took place on the continent to such an extent that the hills and mountains were smoothed down to a fairly level plane. The material thus removed was spread out in shallow inland seas.

Just as there are two chief kinds of rock, the water which figured so largely in the ultimate appearance of our landscapes is of two kinds. One, originating within the earth, is called juvenile. The other, coming from the skies, is named meteoric.

Juvenile water is actually condensed steam which appears on the earth's surface for the first time. In the Death Valley region it springs from the great fault that apparently formed the west face of the Funeral Range. In its egress to the surface it acquires various mineral contents and reaches the surface at an average temperature of about 80°, regardless of season. The copious flow that furnishes irrigation and hydro-electric power to Furnace Creek Inn and Ranch and National Park village and headquarters all comes from this same source.

The water from springs in Trail, Hanapaugh, and Willow Canyons on the opposite side of Death Valley is cool and practically free from mineral content, having come from melted snow and rain in the mountains. This, obviously, is meteoric water, as is all water originating from cloud formations.

Water and rocks join in a common story that you may read just where the Twenty Mule Team Drive leaves Furnace Creek where a slab of stratified and rocklike, hardened mud has well-delineated ripple marks left there by water. In intervening aeons the mud has been consolidated by pressure and later still tilted so that it is exactly 90° from its original angle.

Whatever effect water may have had on their placing or their conformation, the articulate rocks which tell the story of the Valley are not found in chronological order, but rather in wild disorder with older rocks tossed madly on top of younger ones, indicating the uproar that took place in the remotely distant, though not so silent, days.

Just how distant were these days?

Scientists tell us that the first chapter of geological history began at least a billion and a half years ago and some of the rocks of that period, among the oldest known anywhere in the world, are exposed in various places in the Panamint, Funeral, and Black Mountains. Dull-colored, they consist mostly of gneiss, schist, quartzite, and marble, though originally they may have been limestones, shales, sandstones, and granites, subsequently changed by the alchemy of time and the potent forces that worked on them.

Much younger limestones, shales, and quartzites of the second, or Algonkian, period are found on either side of the Valley, near its southern end; youthful as compared with the

63

rocks of the first period, these are still some seven hundred million years old, and it is probable that the first one-celled life on earth appeared while they were being deposited, as curious markings in them may have been due to algae.

Somewhat north of the central part of the Valley the mountains on either side are made up largely of rocks of the third chapter of geological history, although in many places these are covered by products of later periods. A large part of these third-chapter, or Paleozoic, rocks are limestones, indicating that for tens of millions of years this area was intermittently beneath the sea. Substantiating this are the fossils of marine shellfish and plants found in the rocks.

Not much evidence seems available of what transpired during the fourth (Mesozoic) period. That Age of Reptiles, starting nearly two hundred million years ago and lasting for perhaps one hundred and twenty-five million years, was an era of ferns and cone-bearing trees. There were no flowering plants such as we have now and there were apparently no mammals of any kind, but forests of ferns and cone-bearing trees and cycads flourished for the dinosaurs to feed upon.

The rocks of this reptilian age are not well represented so far as is known, so the geologic story of this long period of time is scant, though Triassic limestones are frequent in the Charleston Mountains and Triassic lavas in the south end of the Inyo Range. However, it is evident that granites were forced up through older formations at that time, and an exposed area of granite is encountered today in the Panamint Mountains immediately north of Towne's Pass and south of Wildrose Canyon.

Properly named the Age of Mammals and Flowering Plants, the fifth, or Cenozoic, period might also be called the Age of Tumult in Death Valley. While the preceding periods were by no means static, this one seems to have surpassed all others in its profound earthquake movements which folded, faulted, tilted, and twisted the strata to produce the bewildering effects that exist today.

In this era of chaos Death Valley itself was born when mighty faults and down-warping created the trough that became the Valley. It is an offspring not of erosion, like the Grand Canyon, but of internal disruption.

The tremendous earth movements of this period produced a geological structure so complex and chaotic it is extremely difficult for even an expert structural geologist to understand it and still more difficult to interpret it. The first movements or earthquakes were unique. Instead of blocks slipping upward or downward, which is the usual accompaniment of earthquakes, huge slabs, miles in extent, were pushed laterally toward the west and produced what is known in Death Valley as the Amargosa Overthrust.

W. B. McDougall of the National Park Service writes of this phenomenon:

We can get some idea of what happened if we take two playing cards, lay them on a table end to end, and then push one toward the other. If we push hard enough the card we are pushing will eventually slip either over or under the other card and lie as one shingle lies over the next one on a roof. In the case of the Amargosa Overthrust, however, the cards are composed of great thicknesses of rock and there are more than two of them because there are known to be at least three of these overthrust plates which were pushed toward the west for many miles. Whether these three overthrust plates represent three distinct series of movements, possibly separated by several million years, or whether they all took place simultaneously, is not yet clear, but they, together with some other lateral movements, actually shortened the surface of the earth here by as much as fifty or seventy-five miles.

Following the Amargosa Overthrust movements, folding or wrinkling of the whole crust of the earth by lateral compression forces folded the old thrustfault planes, Dr. McDougall explains, as well as the rock layers themselves and produced a series of ridges and troughs running north and south. One of these troughs was the original Death Valley and the mountains on either side are two of the original ridges.

There is evidence of two distinct periods of folding, one taking place soon after the thrust faulting already described. Between this and the second folding there existed a period of some several million years of erosion during which valleys were cut and mixtures of rocks, gravel, and sand deposited. The second period of folding then cut the old troughs deeper, and forced the ridges higher. And at the same time perplexity for geologists was added by the fact that some of the axes of new folding were at oblique angles to the axes of the old folding!

In his admirable book, *Desert Country,* Edwin Corle gives a graphic picture of this concentrated chaos, together with some comparisons of his own which help to make it understandable.

There were earthquakes beyond belief. There was folding and faulting and tilting; there was igneous intrusion and erosion and alluvial overflow; there was volcanic action and consequent lava and mud. The substance of the earth's surface in this spot was breaking and smashing and fusing, broken down into its constituents and reassembled in new forms. In all this hurly-burly certain ambiguous and dramatic events, geologically at least, were taking place. For example, at Dante's View, which almost everyone visits at some time or other, there is Tertiary rhyolite in direct contact with Archean gneiss. How this came to be can be suggested by visualizing the city of New York today. Suddenly there is a terrific cataclysm, blowing all the city to atoms which are later reassembled at the spot where the cataclysm left them. New York is now made up of the same substance as before—but the Aquarium is in Radio City; Grant's Tomb is in Queens; the Chrysler Building stands where it always did, but its tower is on a garage in Harlem; the Holland Tunnel goes to Staten Island and Brooklyn Bridge spans the Hudson River. If you were to go to New York and discover that these changes had happened in your absence you would be amazed, to put it mildly —and a geologist is equally moved at Dante's View when he discovers Tertiary rhyolite and Archean gneiss—to him the Chrysler tower on a garage in Harlem.

The oddities of Death Valley do not stop even here. Suppose our New York cataclysm reassembled parts of various buildings into a brand-new building made up of Macy's basement, Café Society, Childs Restaurant, the Yale Club, and Mills Hotel, topped off by the penthouse of the Sherry-Netherland holding the Statue of Liberty's torch. Coming upon this mixture, we would certainly look twice. And as we stare a vehicle goes by which is a Fifth Avenue bus at its front end but fuses into a Lenox Avenue subway express at its rear. A geologist finds somewhat analogous incongruities in the Black Mountains, where rocks of eras widely separated in geological time, such as Archaeozoic and Tertiary and Palaeozoic, all combine to form one mountain range.

That, it seems to me, gives the general idea, for scientist or layman.

To add to the confusion, much normal faulting—the vertical slipping up or down of rock masses—took place after the folding. And to top it off (literally) volcanic activity pushed lava rocks into all the cracks and crevices between the rock masses in addition to spilling out onto the surface.

All this folding and faulting and volcanic activity produced depressions of various sizes in the surface, which became lakes. The lakes in turn filled up with sediment running to hundreds of thousands of feet in thickness so that today we see light-yellow or gray or cream-colored deposits where the beds of ancient lakes once were.

It is in the rocks formed from the mud around these lakes that many interesting fossil tracks are found of camels, horses, and other mammals. As a rule the last deposits in an inland lake without outlet, as such a lake dries up, are mineral salts, such as borax or table salt. Characteristically, the borax deposits of Death Valley are found within these lake beds. The vastness of the natural wealth packed beneath the Valley's floor is indicated by the fact that drilling to a depth of 1800 feet was continuously through salt 95 percent pure.

An air passenger between Las Vegas and San Francisco can discern quite plainly that the entire drainage east of the Sierras flowed through a series of now dry lakes—Owens, China, Cuddybuck, Searles Basin, Panamint Valley—and finally through Wingate Pass to Death Valley.*

Even the long, winding Mojave River, originating in the San Bernardino Mountains far to the south, once turned north in the vicinity of Baker, through Silver Lake and on into Death Valley. Indeed, during the floods of the mid-thirties, Silver Lake filled to a depth of several feet and only a low barrier prevented its waters from following the ancient stream bed.

During all this time—a period that corresponds with so countless many years that in comparison our centuries are little more than seconds—what is Death Valley today was no desert, but humid land of near-tropic lushness.

With the coming of the glacial period (about one million years ago) the Valley instead of being paved with dry salt, as now, was filled with water. That ancient lake is now called Lake Manly and its old shorelines can be seen in various

---

* The testimony born by the modern salty fish residents, *Cypridon salinus*, further confirms this. (See Chapter 13).

places, especially on Shoreline Butte in the southern part of the Monument. There were never any glaciers in the Valley itself, although undoubtedly some ice and snow crowned the surrounding mountains during most of the glacial period.

The contemporary building up of the Sierra and the coast ranges in large part is responsible for the progressive drought of Death Valley until today it has the driest climate on the North American continent. Because of this increasing aridity Lake Manly gradually dried up and left the deposit of salt which forms much of the present Valley's floor.

The faulting that started millions of years ago has continued to the present time; occasional earthquakes still occur and the bottom of the Valley is considered a sinking area. Since the end of the glacial period, some twenty-five or thirty thousand years ago, continued erosion has produced the beautifully sculptured areas such as Zabriskie Point and Golden Canyon; the great alluvial fans so characteristic of both sides of the Valley have been built up; the sand dunes near Stovepipe Wells have been formed and oxidation has increased the vividness of coloration in many of the rocks.

Death Valley is a geological museum, whose exhibits are scarcely catalogued.

Donald Curry, who as the Monument's Park Naturalist was this institution's curator for six years, calls it the most remarkable assemblage of geological phenomena to be found in any like area. Almost the whole of recorded geologic time is represented in the Valley itself and its surrounding ranges. Those barren mountains, unclothed by vegetation and with little or no surface debris, give up their secrets as more modest lands cannot.

Even a cursory acquaintance with them must stimulate anyone at all interested in the wonders of Creation.

8. Indians Today

SHOSHONE Johnnie, whose acquaintance you made in the opening pages of this book, often is at and about Furnace Creek Inn, ready enough to dispense his lore to those of proper approach.

There were other notable native characters in the Valley, unhappily most of them now departed to the Happy Hunting Grounds.

Best-known was Indian George, sometimes called Panamint George. At his death in 1944, he was well over a hundred years old. Vital statistics are sketchy when an Indian reaches back that far, but we do know that this patriarch was in his teens in 1849.

Indian George was named, or named himself, after Dr. S. G. George who headed a prospecting party into the Valley in October, 1860. Indian George was perhaps in his early twenties then, and for a time became attached, however informally, to Dr. George's menage. Probably the attachment stemmed from a lively appreciation of what approximated tin-can food in those days and like delicacies.

70

A second gastronomic hanger-on of the George party was Hungry Bill, another Indian who became a fixture in subsequent Death Valley chronicles.

Indian George had his ranch on the western slope of the Panamints, on the fringe of the Panamint Valley a few miles from Ballarat. There, for half a century, he raised goats and basked in the fame that came because he alone of all surviving Indians had seen the dawn of white man's history in Death Valley.

Indian George was alive the first time I traveled from Lone Pine to visit Panamint Valley.

Roundabout there was much else, by some standards more worth seeing than the old Indian. As for instance, the sites of long-dead Panamint and Skidoo, camps once famous in mining history, their civic bones picked bare by the curious competing with the encroaching sands and the desert sun. Or Telescope Peak with its stupendous panorama of this world's weirdest region, fashioned in geological crucibles a million years ago.

But to me, the company of Indian George seemed more urgent than views or ghost towns, for the one would be there always, and ghosts would never be more defunct; while Indian George already was well, though hazily, over a hundred years old and correspondingly impermanent. This ancient Indian of Panamint was the only living person who actually saw the first white men who stumbled through the tortures of Death Valley.

George was a small boy that December day in 1849. He and his father, from a hillside near what came to be called Emigrant Spring, watched the Jayhawker party which had trekked over deserts and mountains all the roadless way from Salt Lake City. Probably just a day or two before, they had

71

burned their wagons to smoke the meat of their starved oxen down in Death Valley.

Two groups of those same Jayhawkers, after forty more days of heartbreak, eventually struggled across the Mojave Desert to the San Francisquito Ranch near what is now Newhall, arriving there February 4, 1850. Today you may drive the distance in four or five comfortable hours.

Indian George, in his long life, told the story of that December morning many times. In the earlier years he had it that the "men with hair on their faces" and the "horned beasts" —never before had he seen white men with their beards, or oxen either—went westward up Emigrant Canyon, where a fine oiled road now runs.

Later, questioned by Superintendent Goodwin, George admitted that actually those three men he saw followed the next canyon to the west, which is now known as Jayhawker Canyon. It was only in 1936 that a boulder in this canyon was found with initials, names, and dates scratched upon it, conclusive evidence of the actual route taken.

"Three men, different from Injun. That I see." George searched his memory of ninety years before. "I ask my father what sort that kind. I think he see white man before. I was scared but papa made me lie still so the hairy men no see us."

After that apparently he and his father had some sight of what was left of the oxen down on the floor of the valley. Or perhaps it was their skulls and bones he saw. George spoke, at least, of the beasts with the horns, although he seems never to have glimpsed any of those first hairy men other than the three scouts, or any of their women and children.

No other white men crossed his trail for the next ten years. Then in 1860 came Dr. George's party and the Indian youth, as well as finding a name he held all his long life, found that white men could be companionable.

Indian George, as we talked, seemed more interested in the present (and cigarettes) than in the past that had made him famous. Perhaps he was weary of it, having told his tale so many times.

My companion that morning was a prospector who had lost a horse.

"You know much," he said to Indian George. "You hear anything about my horse?"

"What horse?"

"Pete."

"Oh, Pete horse. Black horse, white foot?"

"That's right."

"Got crooked tail?"

"That's him."

"Got blaze on face?"

"That's the horse."

Indian George appeared plunged in thought.

"Got wild eye?" he asked finally.

"Yes, a bad eye. Where is he?"

George shook his head.

"Dunno. I no see 'um."

The government has built comfortable houses for its wards throughout our country. But an architectural snarl arose when tenants died. An Indian will not take a body out through the door because then the spirit of the departed can return through that same doorway to plague survivors. So they broke open a hole in the wall, pushed the body out, and stopped up the hole, just as they had done since time immemorial with their own hogans, unless, after a death, they deserted the hovel permanently and built a new one.

With white man's houses this practice of punching out emergency exits seemed something short of economical. So some of the modern adobe houses in the Indian communities have a three-foot section of uncemented wall through which a body can be removed and the wall replaced without lasting damage or loss of time. Federal architects found, too, that Shoshone dwellings should face the east and the rising sun, as ancient custom decreed.

Besides such compromises with the past, the new Indian dwellings have the modern comforts of an average modest home, including running water and a bathroom. We were talking of the changing times and I asked Indian George if such innovations were appreciated.

"Pretty good," he said judiciously.

Observing his own rancheree outhouse, I asked another question.

"They like the inside toilets all right?"

George's reply was almost animated.

"You betcha! Cold water run all time. Good place keep butter."

That other pillar of Indian society, Hungry Bill, who stood six feet four and survived his share of dubious adventures, had established himself, complete with large family and a small garden, in a watered canyon on the eastern slopes of the Panamints, in a regal though reasonably primitive principality. From the door of his shack he commanded one of the most magnificent views imaginable over the length and breadth of Death Valley and across mountains and canyons beyond.

Death Valley Scotty has a tale about hospitality at Hungry Bill's—just as there are Scotty stories about every aspect of the countryside. Such tales are as indigenous and universal as the saline deposits and the summer temperatures.

"One time," says Scotty, "I was down Telescope Peak way an' about the middle of the afternoon I got awful sick and thought I'd better get somewhere quick and the only near place was Hungry Bill's.

"So I rode into his camp, and Hungry was there. I told him I was sick and wanted a place to lie down and I wanted his squaw to wait on me. He grunted and pointed over to the corner of the shack where I could throw my bed. I got the bed off my mule, and put it where he told me, and I'm tellin' ya, I was careful to lay with my back close to the wall, where I could keep an eye on him.

"I happened to have along a couple of boxes of good cigars and that night all them Indians was sittin' around, old and young. Two of them oldest boys was as big as Hungry Bill himself, six feet two and four or more. So I took out a cigar and lighted it and I took about three puffs, and here come Hungry's big hand over my face, like a big ham on the end of his long arm. He took the cigar out of my mouth and put it in his own, took about three puffs, and passed it to Mrs. Hungry. She took three puffs and passed it to the oldest boy, and he took his puffs and passed it to the next. And so that cigar went clear down to the youngest, about fifteen of them altogether, till all the family had a smoke.

"Then I took out another cigar and lighted it and took three puffs, and sure enough, the same thing happened. This big ham reached over and took it out of my mouth, put it in his own and took three puffs, handed it to his squaw, and down the line it went.

"Well, sir, I thought if this is going to keep peace in the family, we'll smoke all night. So that's just what happened. I'd keep takin' them cigars out and lightin' them, and Hungry let me have just three puffs, and that's all he took himself, and the family got it. I'll never forget that night, lightin' them cigars and takin' three puffs and seein' that big brown ham come over my head, and never a word said."

The existence of Hungry Bill, with his home, his garden, and, on occasion, Scotty's cigars, was very different from that of his forebears.

Those original residents of Death Valley were called Panamint Indians, an offshoot of the Shoshone Nation. This particular group seems to have been driven from fairer hunting grounds to the north by their more warlike brothers. As befits a people relegated to such a hard land, the Panamints were masters in the art of desert survival. Capable of great endurance, ingenious in the utilization of every edible or otherwise useful plant, eating any animal they could shoot or catch, following the seasons in incessant migration from valley floor to mountain crest, they managed to exist, to be healthy, and, no doubt, to be happy.

Probably in this region there were from a hundred to two hundred of these swarthy, thickset, stoical citizens. Every aspect of their lives was conditioned by the search for food over much the same circuit year after year, following the lines of ripening vegetation. Grass seeds, piñon nuts, and mesquite beans were the chief foodstuffs. Some green-leaved plants were eaten, though repeated washings and boilings were required to remove their bitterness. Lobes of cactus were prepared by rolling them in the sand to remove their spines and then by boiling or drying.

The fleshy prickly-pear lobes were broken off, scoured free of their bristles, and dried for later use. The thorns of the devil's pincushion protect large supplies of seeds, borne in woolly capsules; they were carefully broken out and the seeds kept, fresh and edible for months. Forms of evening primrose, or grasses that are heavy seed bearers, and of the joint-pine shrub all yielded stocks that were winnowed out and crushed to be cooked as well.

Probably the honey mesquite ranked next to the pine nut

76

as a food reliance. Its beanlike pods carry hard seeds, also a sweet and nutritious pulp. The pods are sometimes fed to horses and mules, taking the place of grain. The seeds were crushed for human food.

Seasoning for these supplies offered no difficulty. Salt enough to supply the world was at hand. For sugar there was the common reed, ready to be cut, dried, sifted, and worked into a sweet gummy mass.

The Indians snared birds and rabbits, or shot them with arrows, and caught mice and lizards of which chuckwallas were the prize, though grasshoppers and grubs were not scorned.

Occasional mule deer were welcome additions to the larder, and the grand prize of all was the bighorn sheep. In campaigns against these crafty animals stone blinds were built and even sizable walls at strategic points to cut off escape. It is interesting to note that in 1891 this wall building was so considerable that white prospectors in the neighborhood became alarmed. The walls were thought to be fortifications, probably preparations for an Indian war or massacre. Eastern newspapers embroidered the tale appropriately.

At various places in and about the Valley obsidian arrowheads, mostly imperfect, are found. The Shoshones of today, and apparently of yesterday, made no pottery, but shards of crude pots, probably obtained from other tribes, have been found at many of their old camps. The women still weave baskets from split shoots of willow and sumac, and decorate them with black from the pods of the unicorn plant. The red used in some of the coarser baskets comes from the roots of the Joshua tree, which grows south and west of Death Valley. In the past, cooking baskets were lined with piñon pitch, red-hot rocks being thrown into water to make it boil.

Among the handiwork of old-time Indians—about which

77

their descendants of today seem to know little or nothing—are the "writings," in this area mostly scratched on soft rocks and called petroglyphs, encountered in a few places throughout the Monument. There are also the unexplained "rock maps" laid out with lines of stones, one of them described in Chapter 17.

In 1849 Manly and his party, then east of Death Valley, came upon an Indian garden of sorts. The meager crop included a vegetable which Manly called a squash, probably the gourdlike growth known as the desert apple or coyote melon.

That patch of foodstuff was the cause of much grief to the travelers, who robbed it.

The immediate result of the vandalism was an Indian attack. Three oxen were shot with arrows, and one of them had to be killed. No doubt word of the white men's bad desert manners preceded them, so that for the rest of the hard journey open Indian hostility was added to the natural perils.

As to Indian food, Manly reported that in caves, probably east of Furnace Creek, the party found—

balls of glistening substance looking like pieces of variegated candy stuck together. The balls were as large as small pumpkins. It was evidently food of some sort and we found it sweet but sickish, and those who were so hungry as to break up one of the balls and divide it among the others, making a good meal of it, were a little troubled with nausea afterward.

While the travelers stole property that was the Indians'—white men have done just that in all quarters of the world, sometimes, as in 1849, because they were truly hungry, often from blind devilment—they ignored food which would have sustained experienced desert dwellers, because they were ignorant of it.

When the emigrants camped at or near Bennett's Wells, for instance, the mesquite trees nearby were laden with nutritious pods. Not far away was cactus that could be eaten. Higher in the hills were piñon pine nuts. And even more important, in the canyons of the Panamints, only a few short miles distant, was running water and grass for oxen.

But the white men did not know what the Indians knew, and some of them, at one place and another, perished, and their stock, too.

In later years, when the tides of civilization had entirely engulfed them, many Indians who did not know and could not contrive to learn what the white men know, in their turn perished. Or, at best sank to sadly low levels of existence.

But not Hungry Bill, Indian George, Shoshone Johnnie, and such as they. Outwardly they were able to change, at least superficially refurbished to cope with their shifting environment. Inwardly, they probably changed not at all, and didn't want certain aspects of their living to change either.

Once I was in Rudie Henderson's store in Lone Pine when he was demonstrating an electric washing machine to an Indian customer obviously entranced with it. Even when Rudie was called away to answer the phone the Indian could not let the machine alone. He'd stick his hand in it and momentarily I expected to see brown fingers taken off by the whirling paddles.

"Well," said Rudie, returning, "do you want it?"

"Uh-uh." The Indian shook his head. "Fine machine. John no like."

"But why not?"

"I look. No good. Make-um squaw heap lazy."

The mentality of an Indian moves in ways peculiarly its

own, and, I think, alters little no matter how the world about him conducts itself. Once I saw an Easterner afflicted with a social conscience encounter the aboriginal state of mind head-on.

It was at Keeler, beside Owens Lake. As we waited in the shade of the little store for a man who was to take us to his talc mine, we watched an Indian arrive on horseback, followed by a squaw on foot. The Indian bought his groceries, put them in a gunnysack, and loaded the pack on the back of the woman. Then he got on his horse for the ride home.

My friend with the conscience didn't like that. Before I realized what he was up to, he stepped out to the Indian the way you'd approach a man who was kicking a child on Park Avenue.

"Look here," he expostulated, "what's the big idea? You riding a horse and your wife walking and carrying everything."

The Indian regarded my friend stolidly.

"Squaw no got horse," he said.

9. Outdoor Hothouse

*A*ROUND Darjeeling, in northern India, nature maintains a unique botanical display. From steaming plains rise slopes lush with the emerald carpets of the jungle that merge into forested mountains and finally climb to the ramparts of the Himalayas. There, in a limited horizontal distance, is every altitude and almost every degree of tropic and temperate climate and soil for plants to choose from.

India's outdoor greenhouse reaches in height from a thousand feet. It is a spectacular cross-section of the world of growing things.

That, of course, is a humid land. The annual rainfall at Darjeeling's seven thousand feet elevation, midway in the climatic gamut between plain and peak, is one hundred inches.

On the opposite side of the world, and with most of its natural attributes in absolute reverse, Death Valley is actually an *arid* replica of this humid horticultural wonderland, conditioned, of course, by its minute rainfall averaging less than three inches in the Valley proper. At least, the region's unique

81

topography provides zones of altitude for its desert growths as diversified as its Asiatic counterpart, although the variety and comeliness of dry-country plant life is infinitely less, and its characteristics utterly different.

With Death Valley, the altitudes start *below* sea level, and reach up to eleven thousand feet. Within that vertical range, from Badwater to Telescope Peak, you may find almost every growing thing that is indigenous to the American desert.

Superficially, the desert growths make a sorry show compared with the colorful displays of dripping jungles and well-watered temperate hill-lands. But as deserts go, the Gothic architecture of Death Valley provides a laboratory of rich reward for the questing botanist or even the casual observer.

The vertical distance between the sub-sea-level floor of the Valley and the surrounding mountains is more than two miles, and those highlands catch considerable snow in winter, so that there is a comparatively abundant supply of water for spring plants, pretty much in proportion to the altitude.

Thus, with the lowering of temperatures at the higher levels and the increase of moisture, each thousand-foot contour creates a different growing condition at any given date. The blooms climb as if relegated by a sort of seasonal rheostat, and continue, at one level or another, far beyond what their usual span would be if all of a kind had matured in one locality.

In April near Stovepipe Wells a desert sunflower or primrose may already be withered and gone to seed, while five thousand feet higher, on the slopes of Towne's Pass, it is blooming lustily; and still higher, at say eight thousand feet, it is but in bud.

The spread in altitude, temperature, and moisture means that some plants can be found in bloom in the Monument every month of the year, and in the very hot hothouse of the deep Valley itself, between its salt line and the frost line, is a rewarding place to study plants—and animals as well—under extreme desert conditions.

Whatever their composite longevity and the perfections of their individual beauty—which often offset lack of size or frequency—these flowers and bushes of the desert have stern problems of their own, most of them obvious to anyone who has been hot and thirsty.

Lack of moisture in the ground and in the air affects every aspect of plant life in such a place as Death Valley. Their height, shape, and frequency, the nature of their leaves and of their roots, all are fashioned to survive meager rainfall and near-zero humidity.

Plants do not grow close together in the desert because they can't afford to share any of their food and fuel with near neighbors.

The widely spaced shrubs, being completely exposed to the light, are generally round in form. In their search for water, the roots travel far. Some cactus roots, on a plane only a few inches below the surface of the ground, spread for as much as eighteen feet. Mesquite is said to send its roots more than a hundred feet in search of moisture. Mary Austin once wrote that the brains of desert plants are underground and certainly it is there that their battles for survival are chiefly fought.

Plant citizens of the dry places are not tall because height is wasteful of moisture. For its life activities a plant requires a supply of water in its cells constantly. The water is absorbed by the roots, passing up through the stems to be used where needed.

But a plant has to carry on respiration also, just as an animal does, absorbing carbon dioxide from the atmosphere to combine it with water to form sugar and starches. In order that these interchanges of gases may take place there must be minute openings through the leaf surfaces, or sometimes

83

through surfaces of the stems, and water is constantly being lost through these openings. It takes time to transport water from the roots to the top of a plant and the taller the plant, the longer that process requires. When evaporation is as rapid as it is in Death Valley a tall plant could not get water up to the top fast enough to counterbalance the loss, and the top of the plant would dry up and die. So desert plants are all low.

To prosper on the desert even low plants require internal engineering different from that of low plants in humid regions.

All the Death Valley shrubs have relatively small leaves and in most cases the leaves drop off at the beginning of the dry, hot summer. New leaves are not formed until the start of the next rainy season. Some shrubs, such as the Mormon tea, have next to no leaves at all, the ordinary functions of leaves being carried on by the green stems. These adaptations are simply means of reducing the evaporation surface in order to conserve water. It is probable that the entire combined leaf surface of all of the shrubs on an acre of ground anywhere in Death Valley proper would not amount to as much as the leaf surface of a single medium-sized maple tree in Ohio.

The creosote bush illustrates another method of conserving water. It retains its small leaves the year round but their surfaces are covered with a resinous material that resembles shellac. This prevents any loss of water except through the minute pores that are designed for the passage of respiration.

More marvelous even than the shrubs are the wild flowers in their ability to withstand drought. While in bloom, these plants show no special adaptation for desert survival, but most of their existence is spent not as flowers growing and blooming above the desert, but as seeds lying on or under its surface.

The seedlings of the annual herbs, which are the wild flowers, appear in late winter or early spring. They grow rapidly, soon come into bloom, produce their fruits, ripen their seeds, and then die in late spring or early summer. The seeds so produced are thrown onto the ground where they are baked by the exceedingly high summer temperatures. Sometimes they are treated to a summer rain and are practically scalded when the sun comes out after the storm, to be baked again as the soil quickly dries out.

Such rigorous treatment does not injure the seeds. They simply wait for the right combination of moisture and temperature the next spring and then germinate. Or, perhaps, delay for another season if conditions are not right. They are practically indestructible, these desert seeds.

Whatever the persistence of the seeds, and the desert wisdom of the parent plants, there are places on the Valley floor with no growing things at all.

This barrenness is not because of lack of water or lack of food. Usually it is caused by too much salt or too much surface erosion. A plant cannot absorb water from a concentrated saline solution, and except for such specialists as the odd jointed Iodine Bush, Arrow-weed, Cooper bush, and alkali Sacaton, nothing grows close to the salt beds.

Also, a plant cannot exist in a soil that does not remain reasonably quiet; no vegetation can take root in drifting sand surfaces and dunes or light soil or gravel frequently disturbed by water or wind erosion.

There are also areas of considerable size that are neither salty nor subjected to erosion but are almost entirely barren of plants. These are sometimes called "desert pavement." Wind and water acting together have shifted about the pebbles and larger rocks and removed the surrounding sand and gravel until they have settled down and become fitted together in such a way as to form a compact mosaic floor of rock. Water rushes over it during storms but does not penetrate it. It is a rock surface rather than a soil surface and plants will have none of it.

In the gigantic natural laboratory that is Death Valley, evolution—geologic, zoologic, and botanic—is extraordinarily well displayed.

Because of its very nakedness, as has been said, the region's geologic secrets are easier to see than in lands clothed in vegetation and cloaked with the deposits of glaciers and erosion. On view, in one way and another, are the progenitors of modern topography, and of animals and plants as well. At a dozen places Nature invites us to reconstruct a specific chapter in the development of a plant community.

For plants, like people, live in communities of many individuals of several or many different kinds, supplemented with an appropriate quota of animals. Before introducing the flowers, shrubs, and trees you will most frequently encounter in a Death Valley visit, a little look at a plant community in the making and in operation, seems worthwhile. To W. B. McDougall, formerly Naturalist of the Monument, I am indebted for the facts of this detour from a precise recording of the Valley's growing things.

At Mahogany Flat in the Panamint Mountains, there flourishes a pine-juniper community, so called because those two trees are its most conspicuous citizens. Once this was a bare rock surface with no soil and no plants or animals. How came a horticultural community to be established in such an inhospitable place?

The only plants that can grow on bare rock with no soil and no external water supply are certain kinds of lichens, which are not single plants but a combination of algae and fungi growing together. Algae we know as the green scum on stagnant ponds, and fungi as molds and mushrooms. Curiously,
86

although most algae grow in water and most fungi grow in places that are at least moist, when the two combine in the structure that is called lichen, they can survive in almost absolute drought.

The type of lichen that first appeared at Mahogany Flat is crustose lichen, forming a very thin crust on the surface of the rock, looking like a smear of paint, and almost any color. This tenacious pioneer corrodes the surface of the rock so slowly it may take a hundred or even a thousand years to prepare enough dustlike soil to support the next arrival.

The second type of lichen resembles foliage and is called a foliose lichen. Foliose lichens continue the corrosion of the rock surface and have body enough to catch particles of wind-blown dust.

After another long time-lapse enough soil is formed to accommodate the third type of lichen, known as fruticose, because of its upright fruiting "branches." Along with this third tenant come the true mosses.

Thereafter the building of soil accelerates though still the time units may be reckoned in centuries. Some plants die and add their bodies to the soil, and finally grasses and small flowering plants gain a foothold. With these larger plants enveloping the rocky surface the building continues until there is enough soil, and sufficient moisture in the soil, to support shrubs and finally trees.

Thus did bare rock evolve into woodland.

Concurrently with this plant development was a comparable evolution of animal life so that the mature community embraced not only many different kinds of plants but many varieties of mammals, birds, reptiles, and insects, all living together.

In a human community man is the dominant organism, determining in a great measure what other organisms may live with him, such as horses, dogs, cats, mice, and flies as well as trees, shrubs, grasses, and flowers. Man doesn't particularly care for mice and flies, but they are present because man is controlling the environment in such a way as to make it a congenial place for them, too.

In our pine-juniper community the trees are the dominant organisms, controlling their environment almost as completely as man controls his. In the same way they determine what neighbors may share the community with them. Here again the other organisms are present not necessarily because they benefit the trees. Parasitic fungi and destructive insects, for example, are counterparts of the unwanted flies and mice of the human establishment.

In a human community there is a definite division of labor, the individual members specializing in various activities. Our pine-juniper community has a comparable technique. The green plants manufacture food for both plants and animals. Some mosses and other low growths have the function of forming a ground cover to prevent too great loss of water from the soil. Certain organisms act as scavengers to get rid of the dead bodies of both plants and animals.

In such a plant and animal community the various resident organisms get along well with each other. There is a nice balance between the plants and the animals, between hosts and parasites, between predators and prey. That condition is called the balance of nature, a balance that must remain undisturbed if the community is to prosper.

No single species of either plant or animal can be removed from such a community without setting up a whole series of disturbances, so interdependent are the residents one upon the other.

Preservation of this balance of nature is a cardinal requirement of the National Park administration. Comparatively far from man-made contamination, its remoteness and the physical conformations of the area make the Death Valley Monument peculiarly self-contained. As such it is a unique showcase of what Nature can do if left to her own devices.

In the Valley, impartial protection is given every native species of both plants and animals. If coyotes and bobcats are killed, rabbits and rodents increase beyond their means of sustenance. If the grass is grazed beyond the requirements of the community population, the wild mountain sheep perish.

Conversely, just as disturbing to nature's balances as decimating a certain animal or native forage, is the introduction of exotic species. Perfect examples of the harmful interloper are the wild burros who eat food the mountain sheep require. They are descendants of animals escaped from prospectors or let loose on the desert, a plague bequeathed by man himself. To avoid such plagues, every living thing which is not truly of the country itself is rigidly excluded.

Everything but man.

Man is still an animal. He is born, he grows, develops, matures, reproduces, and finally dies just as any other animal. But he differs from other animals in his habits. His everyday living is a vastly complex undertaking. Even his traveling is on wheels instead of by the natural method used by all other animals.

Primitive man, existing from the fruits of his immediate environment, was a native of the plant and animal community in which he lived. Modern man is native to an artificial environment that he has largely constructed for himself. Definitely he is exotic to any natural community, and destructive to its balances.

However, exotic and a nuisance as you are, you who read this book, you are privileged because Death Valley National

Monument exists solely for *your* pleasure, recreation, and education.

Therefore in the Parks and Monuments there are roads and trails, hotels and auto camps. In Death Valley you will note that these conveniences have been provided with a minimum of disturbance of natural conditions. Once away from the roads or the resting places, the countryside is almost exactly as it was when white men first saw it in 1849.

You are, in short, a privileged interloper—the only one admitted—in a natural desert community. The next chapter seeks to describe briefly some of the plants you will encounter there.

10. Plants of the Desert

ACCORDING to the admirable check-list completed in 1945 by W. B. McDougall, Park Naturalist, there are 608 different kinds of plants growing in Death Valley National Monument. This list and, indeed, most basic facts about plant residents, is based on the collections made by M. French Gilman, often referred to as the "Dean of Desert Botany."

However, Mr. McDougall adds, "a former check list prepared by W. E. Shanteau contains approximately 650 specific names. So far as records available are concerned, therefore, the number of plant species is probably somewhere between 600 and 700."

Whatever its ultimate total, the extent of the vegetation is remarkable in this hottest and driest of all our deserts.

Plants which flower, of course, are the favorites of the usual visitor. And the delight of wildflower coloring and gay blossoms is enhanced by the contrast of the drab desert background.

In a good "wet" year—with a rainfall of, say, three inches—

the sight of some areas of the Valley floor is lovely indeed. The best of the desert flower-show is apt to be in the northern reaches of the Valley where the road follows its western flanks toward Grapevine Canyon and Scotty's Castle. In April the gray expense of the alluvial fans—those gradual slopes of rock and gravel washed down from the mountains, spreading over the lowlands like opened fans whose handle is the canyon they emerged from—is carpeted with color.

One must see, to believe, how the desert sunflower, in a generous season, fills the eye with its gold, a radiant banner spread wide upon the drab countryside. Each little wash is like a separate gilded rivulet flowing down the slopes toward the glistening salt flats. Only when you pause by the wayside to look closer do you detect the less numerous blooms of the tiny flowers that carpet the gravelly floor. All blend in harmonious patterns of color, less spectacular than famed flowery showspots of California, such as that fabulous panorama of purple lupine viewed from the Grapevine on the way to Bakersfield, but peculiarly satisfying in their delicate perfections.

Among the gay annuals which bloom so briefly in this outdoor hothouse are the fragile primrose, the mallows—"Chinese Lantern" and Spotted—desert heliotrope, tiny gold poppies, and lavender clusters of sand verbena. Tucked among the rocks is the low-growing desert star, a white daisy whose close relative is the taller desert ghost.

Those with sharp eyes will find the mariposa lilies near Harrisburg Flat, and near Mahogany Flat, giant lupine, six feet or more in height, an altogether surprising neighbor to the desert just below. As indeed are also the Panamint daisies whose yellow petals decorate Wildrose Canyon as late as June.

Along the washes is the turtleback plant, which looks like a rounded clump of gray-green coral and smells like turpentine. The purple blossoms of the loco-weed, and the bright red of the scarlet mimulus are found on the upper slopes, while the phacelias, about fifteen varieties, grow in nearly all the washes. So do the nine or ten different species of wild buckwheat, the erigonum. Notable among them are the terraced "Stack-o'-Hots" and the "Cigarette-holder" with its inflated stems.

Viewed in the right perspective, the tawny buckwheats hold delightful possibilities. Many of the varieties remarkably resemble miniature trees. Though they stand only from a few to perhaps eighteen inches above the ground, groups of them seem like tiny replicas of full-sized forests. In some slant-lighted "grove"—it may be a woodland of only a square yard —put the lens of your camera on the ground close beside the tiny "trunks" and with luck your photograph will disclose a strangely lovely forest, its individual broad-branched, flat-topped "trees" oddly reminiscent of the acacias, so characteristic of African veldts.

To some, loveliest of all dry-land growths is desert holly. These compactly branching bushes, from one to three feet high, are rounded silvery bouquets decorating harsh environments. The undulant, sharp-pointed leaves are silver, gray, and olive in varying pastel shades. The "flowers," small berry-like clusters, range from cream color and tan to brick-red, the males different from the females. In an area of an acre Ted Ogston and I found plants of six distinctive shades both of leaf and flower, and made a color photograph to refresh the memory of their infinite and intimate variety. Holly is of the saltbush tribe, hardy desert folk tolerant of very dry, and alkaline, soils.

The creosote bush is as characteristic of the American desert as bluegrass is of Kentucky or elms in New England. However, the floor of Death Valley lacks creosote, although in higher areas of the Monument the ubiquitous bush is dominant, as elsewhere on the desert. The abundant growths of the Valley proper are mesquite, saltbush, arrow-weed, and the lovely desert holly.

Most seen of the Valley's trees, mesquite grows in thickets, tinting the bottoms of washes with the olive-green hue of its much-divided leaves. Where the mesquite flourishes, no matter how dry the adjacent sands may seem, somewhere not far below is water.

Mesquite makes up in usefulness what it lacks in beauty. For many an Indian and rancher its wood has supplied shelter, furniture, firewood, and fencing. Food, too, for the beans from its branches often made meals when ground in metates fashioned from its hollowed trunk. Rodents relish the seeds from those beans, storing them for winter. Bees harvest the honey during mesquite blossom time. Coyotes like the beans, too. Some say these animals are chiefly responsible for the widespread seeding and reseeding of mesquite—an interesting sidelight, by the way, upon the functioning of our plant-and-animal community, and its natural balances.

The creosote bush, lacking the mesquite's versatility, has at least a wider desert distribution. Its slender stems covered with brown bark and bright green leaves, glossy with a sort of varnish, are everywhere about the desert excepting only the sub-sea-levels of Death Valley. Its delicate flower is yellow and is apt to appear at any season, following a rain. The creosote is sometimes called covillea, in honor of Dr. Frederick Vernon Coville who in 1891 made the first botanical study of the Valley.

The aromatic fragrance of burning creosote twigs to many desert enthusiasts is as pleasing as the sweetly perfumed smoke of sagebrush campfires, or even the pervading scent of growing sage after new rains. For the desert places, I suppose,

94

these two bring the same sort of contented memories that the aroma of balsam, hemlock, or pitch pine conjure up for campers of the mountains and the Eastern forests.

In well-watered canyons of the Monument cottonwoods and even willows are found. Piñons, whose nuts were important in Indian economy, grow on the highlands of the Panamints and the Grapevines. Above five thousand feet, too, is the locale of the pine-juniper community with its bristlecone and limber pine, as well as juniper. Thereabouts some Rocky Mountain maple is encountered and much sturdy mountain mahogany, its wood so heavy, hard, and tough a sledge is sometimes a better weapon against it than an ax. As some of us know to our grief, weathered dead trunks will dull the edge of a saw almost as effectively as nails.

The rust-red bark of the mahogany was the basis for a dye made by the Indians, who found uses for many desert plants. Squaw cabbage, the tuber-like roots of which were edible after repeated washings, was a food plant. The straight stems of the arrow-weed, which grows in peculiar wind-blown clumps which give the name to the Devil's Cornfield, produced shafts for arrows. Still others furnished dyes, wood for bows, utensils, and ornaments.

Among the desert plants-of-several-uses is ephedra, variously called squaw tea, mormon tea, desert tea, Mexican tea. By any name it makes a delicious beverage.

Several varieties abound in many Southwest desert regions, and ephedra *Funerea*—that is, of the Funeral Mountains—is widely distributed in the Monument. Incidentally, several kinds also are resident of the Mediterranean Basin, China, and South America.

Of the Death Valley brand of tea, French Gilman once wrote: "How odd it is that in the original description no mention was made of the shape of the bush. It is really very symmetrically rounded and does not sprawl out. The gray-green branches are in general shorter than in other species, and radiate from definite centers on the main stem."

Added to its other virtues, ephedra, and especially *Funerea,* is a pleasing addition to the landscape. Aside from the Death Valley variety, generally it is a rather straggling bush, usually low but sometimes attaining a height of five feet. It has slender, erect, broomlike branches, with long-jointed fluted stems which seem bare because the papery leaves are minute and soon shed. The prevailing colors, dependent upon locality, range from the bright green of the plants of higher altitude, through yellowish olive to smoky gray. Surprisingly, ephedra is of the joint fir family (*Gnetaceae*), closely related to the pines, the male and female blossoms being actually cones.

Indians, pioneers, Mormons, Mexicans—and those friends who have tried it—like the tea ephedra makes. There is no trick to its concoction. Simply boil a handful of the stems. Long boiling does not make for bitterness, and some experimentation will demonstrate the strength you like best. A thick brew can be kept and later diluted for iced desert tea. Sugar, with lemon or cream, becomes the beverage quite as well as in the imported product. In the making, some prefer to use green stalks, others dry, and there is field for choice among the varieties of the plant itself, although I can detect no difference in the flavor. A supply may be kept indefinitely. After a year of storage I have found the stems quite as potent and as palatable as when first picked. Outside the Monument on any of its approaches, there are thousands of bushes to yield the few twigs you'll want for a first trial.

In the stems of ephedra is tannin. The beverage made from it was largely used by Indians and old-timers as a remedy for colds, fevers, and intestinal disorders, and it is said to figure in present-day pharmacopoeia. But beyond its medicinal properties ephedra makes a delicious beverage and one with which some experimental marketing is apparently contemplated. Perhaps the fragrant desert tea will become another sort of desert gold, just as borax did!

Cactus is the most characteristic of all desert growths. Cactus and deserts are as inseparable as ham and eggs, and Death Valley Monument is well provided.

Although cactus is indigenous to America, the Greeks had the word for it, *Kaktos*, meaning "a kind of prickly plant." And by the way, when you speak of plural cactus, the word may be either "cacti" or "cactuses."

All plants that have thorns are not cacti, and all cacti do not have thorns. Some have fierce spines and others are soft and feather-like. In size they range from the giant sajuaro, towering fifty feet high, to diminutive button cactus. Gorgeous flowers, large and small, are white, yellow, and all the warm shades from delicate pastel pink to flaming crimson.

Cacti, for the most part, live in hard country and have special equipment for survival. Protective features found in varying degrees in different species, are: The surface exposed to evaporation is scant. The skin is thick and tough, with pores sunk in its surface. The skin has a waxy covering. The surfaces are ribbed and fluted, permitting an accordion-like expansion and contraction proportionate to the water supply. There are special tissues for water storage. Complex root systems are designed for finding and keeping moisture, for cacti alone of all desert plants actually hoard water. The spines provide shade as well as protection, like a lath house. Canny citizens of the desert are the cacti.

Cactus is an American institution, descendant of some group of leafy plants which once thrived in jungles bordering

97

the lakes that often preceded the deserts we now know. To-day, by and large, its happiest habitat is Mexico. However, only three states in the union have no cactus: Maine, Vermont, and New Hampshire.

Death Valley's cacti most frequently encountered are beaver tail, cholla, finger, fishhook, grizzly bear, hedge hog or cotton ball, niggerhead, pineapple, prickly pear, and straw-berry. Of the lot, niggerhead, beaver tail, and cholla, princi-pally, bloom brilliantly, as does the strawberry cactus, whose blossoms are succeeded by a delicious fruit, well protected by sharp spines.

Most spectacular of desert plants is the yucca, and most grotesque its relative, the Joshua tree.

The Mojave yucca, or Spanish dagger, while not itself in-digenous to the Monument, is often seen along the desert roads that lead to Death Valley. Yucca flowers are gorgeous clumps of white and palely yellow blossoms clustered on long stems that rise from the central cup of pointed, trough-like leaves, yellow-green and dagger-sharp. The yucca's showier neighbor is parry molina, with which it often is confused. This resident of rocky hillsides has golden-white flower stalks a foot in diameter at their base and often twelve feet high. A forest of them in flower is the loveliest sight imaginable, and viewed by moonlight the ghostly blooms, like towering pale candles, beggar description.

In the Monument, Joshua trees grow in the higher altitudes of the Grapevine Mountains. Throughout the neighboring Mojave Desert, these sturdy prickly trees are as characteristic of the countryside as elms in New England. They do not bear their greenish-white blooms every year, the interval between the times of flowering being governed by vagaries of rainfall and temperature. The height of the trees is from twenty to thirty feet, their branches wide and often deformed in strange angular patterns, which give them personalities peculiarly their own. Edmund Jaeger tells us that from the spreading disklike base of the trunk great numbers of small roots penetrate both downward and horizontally, providing moisture and anchorage against gales.

As ghostly as the flowering yuccas, and far more weird, are the odd contorted silhouettes of the Joshuas seen at night. All over the deserts they stand solitary against the skylines.

There were times when the trees, which somehow seem so ancient and so weary, were fiery symbols. Then you might see them marching toward the horizon, those near, pillars of fire, the distant ones pin-points of light in the purple night. For the Indians, when one died, set out the young men to light a long straight row of beacons, one Joshua tree after another, so that there was a bright clear way to the edge of this world for the spirit of the departed to follow as it set out to find the world of eternity that waited.

11. Death Valley Scotty

I_N the past thirty years Death Valley Scotty has had about as much attention as Death Valley itself. Visitors ask as many questions about him as they do about the heat they've heard of. He is another superlative. Just as Badwater is the lowest place in America, Scotty's stories are the tallest.

Scotty's Castle is one of the authentic wonders of the West. So also, in a more moderate measure, is Scotty's partner, Albert M. Johnson, a former Chicago businessman who pays the bills and likes it.

The relation between Johnson and Scotty always reminds me of Bergen and Charlie McCarthy. Scotty, though no dummy, was the front man who did the talking. With Johnson's blessing and Johnson's cash, he swaggered to his heart's content. In some oblique way Johnson extracted his million— or several million—dollars' worth of vicarious fun from the show, which for a dozen years was incomparable.

I use the past tense, because life at the Castle and abroad is less sensational than in the gilded days when Scotty scattered

100

currency like Mardi Gras confetti, hired a special train to set a record from Los Angeles to Chicago, and produced Aladdin riches from mythical gold mines. Age, financial losses, and law suits which pricked some of the iridescent bubbles, have had their subduing effect.

Scotty on occasion drank and swore on a magnificent scale, rolled his own, took proper pride in his reputation as a monumental creator of fiction. Johnson neither swore, drank, nor smoked. Though he had a juvenile zest for wearing six-shooters and frontier regalia, this white-haired, fine-featured gentleman was content to remain mysteriously silent, the sphinx of Grapevine Canyon, while his well-heeled court jester wove the exaggerations the odd partnership delights in.

To match those two you'd have to team up P. T. Barnum and Baron Munchausen, and even then something would be lacking. Perhaps a dash of Mike Romanoff is the missing ingredient.

I wish that one day Albert Johnson, who is a clever man, would write the authentic story of that partnership. It could be a notable edition to whimsical Americana.

Scotty, or Walter Scott, to use his formal and seldom-heard name, is short, thick, and paunchy with the small feet and hands of a horseman. Shrewd steel-blue eyes are set in a face burned red by years of desert sun. His white hair is hidden by the inevitable high-peaked Stetson.

Scotty is an authentic product of the West, out of Kentucky by Buffalo Bill's circus. He was a trick rider, roper, and shot. He has all the graces of the good bad-man. He knows the answers. Also, he really does know the desert. In all ways he is a magnificent model of what a fictional desert hero should be, in looks, speech, and dehydrated humor.

For some years, now, the Castle has been open to paying guests, who, for a dollar admission fee plus tax, may enjoy a conducted tour, complete with lecture, through its elegances. And, if the visitor is fortunate, also glimpse Scotty himself.

Latterly, however, Scotty sticks pretty close to his home ranch a few miles away. Usually at the Castle they'll tell tourists he is ill. Laid up from the effects of a rattlesnake bite, or perhaps a mule stepped on his foot. There are variations.

Scotty limped into the Castle one evening some years since and solicitous guests crowded around to find out what ailed his leg.

"S'nothin'," Scotty insisted stoically. "Nothin' at all. Just a mountain lion."

"A mountain lion!" the ladies gaped.

"That's it," Scotty admitted ruefully. "Down to my cabin on the lower Vine. I notice the door was part open, and I pushed in sort of slow. It was a bit dark inside but perched on a shelf beside the fireplace I saw a right big lion. That sorta startled me and I stood still to see what he would do. I didn't rightly want to shoot him where he was on account of the mess it would make. Well, that lion gave one jump for the open door. He hit me an awful wallop as he went through and knocked me down. That's how I come to sprain my leg." He rubbed the offending limb thoughtfully.

Some said it was gout, but Scotty said it was rattlesnakes or mules or a mountain lion.

On another occasion I overheard the lecturer telling the tourists about it.

"No," he said, "Scotty doesn't get around much just now. He's laid up at his place. A black widow spider bit him."

A very great deal has been written about Walter Scott and Albert Johnson, their castle, their will-o'-the-wisp mine, their hospitality, and their troubles.

Sifted from the legends, some facts are reasonably clear.

Walter Scott was born in Cynthiana, Kentucky, sometime between 1868 and 1876. The date is elastic. The answer depends upon whom you ask.

Scotty's first job in Death Valley was in the eighties for the borax people, or possibly stake-punching in a government survey party came first. He learned to handle himself in the desert. Later he acquired showmanship and worldly wisdom with Buffalo Bill.

He saw London and Paris. He hobnobbed with the Prince of Wales. Young, breezy, full of devilment, in New York he went to town in a very big way indeed. He became as much at home in Madison Square Garden as he is around Ubehebe Crater today.

It was at the Garden he made Irene Watkins famous. Here is her story as he told it one night at the Castle.

"There was a Dog and Cat Show going on at Madison Square Garden just ahead of our Wild West Show," said Scotty. "A newspaperman I knew told me it wasn't doing very well. So as I wasn't busy I thought I'd see about putting that pet show on the map.

"With my reporter friend I went to a saloon where'd I'd seen a cat hanging around in the alley. It belonged to the saloon. I paid them a dollar for it, and it was a right good-looking cat for an alley cat.

"I knew the manicure girl at the Hoffman House, so I took the cat to her and got her to fix it up. She manicured the cat's nails and put pink color on them, then she washed its fur with Chinese shavings, and that made it stand all out and kind of curl. When she got through with it, that was something special in cats.

"We named the cat 'Irene Watkins.' Then I went to a concern that made fine cages and they give me one of their best.

103

The Wild West Show hadn't begun yet, so I got one of the peanuts-and-popcorn boys who was waiting just like I was, to be an attendant for Irene. One of the best clothing houses in New York give him a uniform, with fancy gold braid on it, and 'Irene Watkins' in gold letters on the collar. He stood beside Irene's cage in the show.

"All the while my friend was feeding this stuff to the papers.

"Then I arranged with a high-class restaurant across the square to have a special waiter bring Irene's meals over to the show regularly, on a silver tray, in one of them silver dishes with a cover on top of it to keep it warm. He'd come across the street, balancing the silver tray over his shoulder. In the dish was fish fins. Irene Watkins would paw them over but seldom eat any. You see, we always give her liver and cream, nights after the crowd was gone.

"Then I got a Fifth Avenue jeweler to make a bracelet, all covered with diamonds, for Irene's left paw. On her right paw we put a big diamond solitaire. Then we rubbed catnip on the bottom of her right foot, and there she'd sit with her left foot down with this wide band of diamonds on it, and she'd be licking her right foot, flashing that big solitaire.

"Well, say! Did the crowds come? That show went on the map. They had to have a special policeman stand by Irene's cage to watch them diamond bracelets and handle the crowd. The manicure girl came over every day and manicured Irene's nails. You never could get near the cage when she was there.

"At the end of the show, the judges gave Irene Watkins a special first prize and me twenty dollars, but the paper came out the next day and said I wasn't keeping the money because the judges was under a false impression. You see, Irene Watkins was a tom-cat and they didn't know it.

"I sold Irene for two hundred dollars and gave the money to

104

the Children's Hospital and the Dog and Cat Show moved out and the Wild West Show moved in."

After his metropolitan experiences, Scotty began profitably combining the arts of publicity with the lures of desert gold.

The story of this period, when one can piece it together, reads like a promoter's Alice-in-Wonderland. Scotty popped up periodically with new tales and fat bankrolls. But no one saw where the cash came from and few seemed to believe Scotty in all his variegated career ever did much mining.

Of that saga there are certain highlights.

The first time he saw Death Valley, Scotty probably was in his mid-teens. He was a cowhand then for John Sparks who later became governor of Nevada, and crossed the deserts chaperoning Sparks' cattle. About 1886 Scotty was driving a borax wagon at the old Harmony works, which still stand some five miles northwest of Furnace Creek Inn. That was the year William T. Coleman, Scott's fellow Kentuckian, whom Dana's New York *Sun* supported for President in 1884, lost the fortune he had made and went broke.

For his part, Scotty went to points East, including New York, where he promoted Irene Watkins and prospered as a showman with Buffalo Bill.

Periodically he was back in the desert, too, enough to get the feel of the mining boom that was boiling in those days, and to garner some good ideas of his own about prospecting and its opportunities.

In 1903, or thereabout, Julian Gerard, brother of James Gerard and then a vice-president of the Knickerbocker Trust Company, equipped Scotty with a fifteen-hundred-dollar grubstake, which subsequently was enlarged. That was a common practice. A grubstaker supported a prospector. If the prospector located ore while the grubstake lasted, he and his backer shared the proceeds. If nothing was found before the grubstake was eaten up, that was that, with no further obligations either way.

The ensuing chapter in Scotty's story is set down by C. B. Glasscock in his extremely entertaining book, *Here's Death Valley*. With the permission of the author's widow, the episode and some of its trimmings, a bit abridged here and there, is quoted:

It is not recorded precisely how long the initial Gerard grubstake to Scott lasted. But after a time Scott appeared in Riverside, California, with a heavy bag, bound with chains, padlocked and sealed, and announced that it contained $12,000 worth of gold amalgam. Riverside is near the edge of the Mojave Desert, only 250 miles from Death Valley. It knew a good deal about mines and miners. It knew that no mine produced gold amalgam, and that no mills were working in Death Valley. It did not get excited, and after a few days Scott picked up the bag and moved on.

For his next publicity release he wisely chose Philadelphia, where he was reasonably certain the public would not know amalgam from high-grade ore. . . . Besides, he had improved his technique. By getting off an eastbound train in Philadelphia and reporting to the authorities that he had been robbed of a sack containing 120 pounds of gold amalgam, he put his own name into national circulation.

"It isn't the loss of the stuff I mind," he was quoted. "I've got a roll left and there is plenty more where the dust came from. But what will the boys say when they hear of it?"

Walter Scott had opened an apparently inexhaustible mine of publicity. But that was not precisely the sort of mine for which Gerard had advanced the grubstake. So Scott found another. . . .

Even Gerard had never seen that mine. The theft of gold reported in Philadelphia had relieved Scott of the necessity of showing Gerard some cashable returns. Gerard wanted to be

106

shown. Scott, robbed of his gold amalgam, needed more money. So, in that impasse, Scott made a deal with one Burdon Gaylord, an eastern mining engineer and promoter who was developing some properties in San Bernardino county. Gaylord advanced several thousand dollars. Scotty promptly supplied publicity.

He arrived at Barstow on his favorite mule from Death Valley in the first week of July, 1905. They knew him in Barstow. His weather-beaten face, his shrewd blue eyes and jovial manner, his huge Stetson and blue flannel shirt and flaming red necktie had been widely publicized from Philadelphia to San Berdoo.

They had seen Scott and Pearl and Keyes go out of Barstow on occasions in the past year with a string of pack mules well loaded with supplies and equipment, including plenty of fire arms, headed for a secret mine in Death Valley. They had even put the story on the wires on one occasion when the outfit included two pigeons, two bobcats, a rattlesnake and a sheepdog. . . .

After a day or two of basking in the warm light of publicity, Scott called upon John J. Byrne, General Passenger Agent of the Santa Fe lines west of Albuquerque. He sailed his sombrero across the office and offered to buy any part of the Santa Fe system that seemed necessary to travel to Chicago in forty-six hours.

In 1905 that was many hours faster than the east-bound run had ever been made. But the Santa Fe understood publicity values as well as Walter Scott. Mr. Byrne figured. After a while he said the train would cost $5,500.

Scott counted out the bills. No other mine has yet been discovered that produces hundred-dollar bills. Scott's wife later went on record as saying that the special train cost $60,000. Scott himself said the trip cost $100,000. But by that time he had a reputation to maintain.

Documentary evidence, revealed by this writer for the first time in print, that the train cost only $5,500, is contained in the photographic reproduction of the railroad's receipt to Scott, signed by John J. Byrne.

The spread-eagle railroad journey was a great success. No cowboy ever before rode so far so fast. Records were broken both in speed and newspaper space. If the words written about that excursion were put end to end they would reach from Rhyolite to Shoshone and back again. The run from Los Angeles to Chicago, 2244 miles, was made in forty-four hours and forty-four minutes. That was thirteen hours faster than the time of the regular Santa Fe Limited of those days.

Not so long ago Scotty gave me a new version of that historic event. We were sitting in the Castle's great hall, deep in seductively leather-lined chairs before the Spanish iron grill screening the baroque fireplace where blazed ties from the defunct Tonopah and Tidewater Railroad.

"We oughta made eight million dollars from that deal," said Scotty. "Y'understand?"

I said I didn't.

"Stock," he explained. "We didn't buy enough. We only made a million. The Santa Fe was in a bad way, y'understand? That publicity was what they needed. A shot in the arm. It put 'em on the map. The public et it up like mountain trout."

He ran his short thick fingers through his long white hair. Obviously he was considering the error he and his partner had made, sharing with me the mortification the memory brought.

"We muffed that one. Get me?"

I thought I did.

That yarn likely was cooked up on the spur of the moment. It was only hospitable to give me something good. And characteristic. That later I was not able to find any movement worth mentioning in Santa Fe stock following Scotty's adventure, is not important.

Anyway, the fifty-five-hundred-dollar train ride seems to have been satisfactory to all concerned. Except Julian Gerard. His reactions appear to have been slightly sour.

The apparent end of the Gerard-Scotty story, which moved forward from that point on through pages whose typography is sometimes misted, came in a postscript when Gerard sued for a half-share of Scotty's take from the mine he said he'd found. The Eastern banker felt, as grubstaker, he had that coming to him from his partner.

But Eastern bankers have been burned before and Mr. Gerard emerged with blisters. So did Scotty's claims to solvency. The pride-puncturing outcome was the court's findings that Scotty had no mine and never had one, unless one could call the generous Albert Johnson such. So there was nothing to divide.

12. Barnum and Munchausen

ABOUT when the first World War was in
the making, Albert Johnson, God's gift to Grapevine Canyon,
came into Scotty's life. Or maybe it was Scotty who hatched
the partnership. Anyway, as a meal ticket the Chicagoan
proved superior to any mine, and more dependable. Also, he
had a zany sense of humor which must have delighted this
cowboy who created Irene Watkins. Then, too, Johnson loved
the desert.

The new partner, equipped with some millions, emerged
from the presidency of an insurance company to set up shop
with Scotty in the desert. He staked his friend in various
fantastic activities whose chief goal, it appears, was to get
themselves talked about and written about. At that they did
well.

The final denouement of the Gerard legal skirmishes came
much later, of course. Not that such judicial determinations
made any difference. Often before, Scotty had been blasted
as being rather less than he claimed to be. But he never seemed
to care, Johnson didn't care, and the public didn't care and

forgot fast. It had hoisted its hero on a pinnacle of sorts, and there it meant to keep him just so long as he put on a good show, which Scotty always did.

Walter Scott, then and now, is an institution, like the Valley itself. Or the Castle. Even if you don't relish desert, or don't like Johnson's brand of architecture, you want to see Death Valley and you want to visit the Castle. So if Walter Scott *is* a modern Munchausen, what of it?

Anyway, the fiction of the mysterious mine was maintained and Johnson let Scotty pose as the owner of the Castle into whose incompleted construction and furnishings went not less than a million dollars and probably much more. Johnson owns and always owned the Castle and apparently has paid for all of Scotty's escapades since they first teamed up.

The most costly of them is Scotty's Castle itself. Although it stands in Johnson's name it is not "Johnson's Castle" and I am sure Johnson never wished it so.

The erection of the Castle started about 1924. It has never been completed and apparently never will be. In any metropolitan area it would be notable. In Hollywood it could grace a super-production motion-picture set, for it is stupendous, colossal, and, in its own way, an epic. But the real wonder of it is its location in a stark and arid wilderness, a madhatter dream come true in a desolate canyon seventy miles from a railroad, with utter desert all around, on the fringe of a neighborhood singularly appropriate for such queer company— Death Valley.

So many things about the Castle are incredible. As, for instance, that it was built on land its owners did not own.

When construction was well under way, Johnson is supposed to have asked Scotty where he kept the deed. But Scotty had no deed. Never had one. So a homestead entry was filed to cover the place they were building on. Unfortunately, it was registered in the wrong township. Another entry was made, but under a new survey it turned out to be some six miles distant from the site it was meant to cover. Before that final act in the Grapevine comedy of errors was caught up with, the land where the budding Castle actually stood had been withdrawn by the President in connection with the pending establishment of the Death Valley National Monument.

Congress came to the rescue then, with a bill permitting Albert M. Johnson to purchase 1529 acres of desert land under and around the Castle at $1.25 an acre.

This time they were the correct acres. Johnson owned the land, all right. But there was question as to who owned the Castle.

That problem was at least approached by a patent filed on July 19, 1938, with the Recorder of Inyo County, California, which conveyed to Johnson the land but reserved to the United States "all minerals the land may contain, together with the right to prospect for, mine, and remove the same. . . ."

It says, too, that if any transfer of all or part of the property occurs, "the Secretary of the Interior shall be authorized to reacquire the land by purchase, condemnation or otherwise."

So it seems that some day Death Valley Monument may have added to its official possessions one Castle, unique, incomplete, and of implausible history.

The name carved on the massive lintel of the door says "Death Valley Ranch," but by whatever name and whatever its future or its past, Scotty's Castle is worth seeing.

Built of concrete, the structure is roofed with red tile, its main building with two units on opposite sides of an oblong patio, both with towers that are topped by wrought-iron weathervanes showing Scotty punching burros across the heavens. A vast, two-storied living room occupied much of the main building, with a huge fireplace at one end facing a fountain at the other. Opening from the interior balcony that overhangs this almost baronial chamber, and as also in the north wing across a causeway, are guest rooms designed and furnished in a grand manner more characteristic of pre-revolutionary Spain than of a place like Grapevine Canyon. The rugs, tapestries, woven curtains, much of the furniture and the carved doors, leather, and iron work, are magnificent. Each bathroom has its special gay tiles, and thousands of other tiles, long ago brought from the Mediterranean to line the swimming pool that never has become more than a pathetic hole in the ground, remain boxed in the cellars. There is a music room, too, with a fine pipe organ, a clock tower with chimes, guest house, stables, workshops; altogether an unparalleled manmade oasis in any desert.

Some say the architecture is a free adaptation of Provincial Spain. Glasscock called it "a rare combination of Moorish, Spanish, Italian, and California Mission." I've written that it seems to hold a trace of Early Hollywood.

One evening on the bookshelves of T. R. Goodwin, Superintendent of the Monument, I chanced upon a volume that obviously had been sent someone to review.

"Oh, that," Goodwin answered my query. "That was Alexander Woollcott's."

Woollcott, it appeared, had donated a considerable number of books to the CCC camp after a visit to Death Valley on New Year's Day, 1936. Some of those books had been inscribed by their authors to Alec, though doubtless that gesture made as little impression upon the ultimate CCC reader as it had upon the Town Crier.

Woollcott was eager to see Scotty's Castle because his admired friend Frank Lloyd Wright had been its architect. At least, so he thought. Goodwin told him that wasn't so; Wright had made the plans but they had not been used. Alec was sure they had been.

"Well, let's go see it," said Alec.

So Goodwin drove with him the fifty miles to Grapevine Canyon, Woollcott recurrently insisting with agreeable firmness that of course he was correct about the architecture.

"He was something to see," said Goodwin. "Especially in that setting. A fabulous figure complete with Homburg hat, theatric cape, and gold-headed cane. Right out of Dickens."

On the road they encountered Scotty and Albert Johnson bound for Furnace Creek. Johnson got out of his car and was introduced to Woollcott. Scotty sat pat.

"I went over to Scotty," Goodwin told me, "and explained who our visitor was. 'An' who in hell might that be?' Scotty wanted to know. He never did get out of the car. When I went back to Woollcott he was palpably crestfallen, for Johnson had told him that Frank Lloyd Wright's plans had not been used."

Actually, Wright had created a lovely design, a modified Hopi structure utterly appropriate to the surroundings, but Johnson shelved it in favor of a conglomeration to his own taste, an architectural mating of Spain and Early Hollywood.

They kept on to Grapevine, but after one look at the Castle Alec would not get out.

"I've seen enough," he said.

The retreat from this esthetic pilgrimage was made in disillusioned silence.

If Woollcott had persisted he might have met Verbena. There was a time at the Castle when you often did. Verbena has a daughter named Daisy. She was likely to show you the scar on top of Daisy's head, especially if Scotty was around.

114

For Scotty was the obstetrician who helped get Daisy born. Without him no doubt there would have been two less Indians in the rancheree. And that scar wouldn't be on Daisy's head.

"Verbena was a right pretty Indian girl," Scotty tells the story. "I never will forget the time when she was living down the canyon in the Indian camp, a few hundred feet from the house. I was alone on the place, except for the Indians. Verbena was due to have a baby that summer. Well, one night Verbena began to holler. I thought I'd go up to the camp and take a slant at things. I saw all the Indians around Verbena's tepee, not doing anything excepting now and then one of them would moan and sing and holler in tune with Verbena. Well, I didn't see as there was anything for me to do, so I went home and went to bed.

"But after midnight, Verbena got to hollering louder and louder, and a lot of them Indians got to singing and yelling, and things grew worse and worse. You see, the baby didn't want to come. I couldn't sleep, there was so much racket. I laid and smoked all night but morning came and things wasn't no better. That baby just didn't want to get born.

"About six o'clock a couple of Indian bucks went into Verbena's tepee to see if they couldn't help things along. One of them got on each side of Verbena and lifted her out of her blankets and put their arms under her shoulders and lifted her up and jumped her up and down. Sakes alive, how she hollered! And all the squaws hollered, and I'm tellin' ya, it was all hell let loose.

"By noon I couldn't stand all that ky-yi-ing any more and I concluded to take a hand. So I got out my biggest jack-knife and I washed it good in the dishpan and I went down to the camp. I told Verbena's mother, 'Now, Dolly, you take this knife, and right on top of the papoose's head is a soft spot and you cut a little slit right in that spot, but be careful, don't cut

115

too deep. Don't cut into the papoose's brain. Then you get your finger under the skull and pull papoose. If papoose dead, throw it away and bring me back my knife.'

"Dolly had a good deal of sense for an Indian, and she did just what I told her, and pulled and the baby was born. Well, Verbena, she stopped yelling right away. She said she was going to call the baby Daisy because she liked flower names and the baby was a girl. Most every time I see them, Verbena pulls the hair apart on top of Daisy's head to show me the scar."

When Scotty finishes the story of Verbena, he is apt to remind his audience what a hard country his country used to be.

"Cruel. That's what it was. An' full of the damnedest surprises," he'd add meditatively, which meant that another story was coming up.

The time I have in mind the yarn was about that mule Scotty had to leave standing in his tracks, all because of an odd freak of some highly mineralized rock.

As our historian states it, he was riding along the top of a narrow ridge. He stopped for a moment to have a look around, but when he was ready to move on, the mule couldn't budge.

"Beatin' him didn't do no good. Seemed like he couldn't lift his feet no matter how hard he tried. That's the first time ever I saw a mule who *looked scared*." Scotty indicated that phenomenon made *him* a bit uneasy, too.

"So, I got off to see what was wrong. I stepped around to the mule's head thinking I might try a blindfold to get him started. An' would you believe it, once my two feet were on that ledge, *I* couldn't move either. They was clamped down tight. After a bit I figured out the trouble. That rock was *magnetized*. The magnetic pull was holding the mule's shoes, an' it had caught hold of the hobnails in my boots, too. So I worked out

116

of my boots. By the time I got back over that trail my stockings were plumb wore out."

"What about the mule?" someone asked.

Scotty showed he felt badly about that.

"The poor critter," he said sadly. "I had to leave him right there. He died, I reckon."

In the days when Scotty's mysterious mine was highly publicized, its owner was often followed, as naturally folks wanted to know the treasure's location. Enough stories stemmed from the sleuthing that resulted to make in themselves a respectable book—at least in bulk.

Scotty established his own "tin-can springs," places where he buried cans of water. He had his fun, it appears, in leading people who trailed him into areas where there was no water at all, except these personal supplies he'd planted. After a couple of dry camps, they'd give up.

One spot in Scotty's hide-out country is still called Poison Spring, because he posted this discouraging notice beside it:

> *"Have just poured five pounds*
> *of arsenic in this spring.*
> *Drink it at your own risk."*

Apparently no one felt like trying it to see if Scotty was fooling.

A little book which Ray Goodwin found years ago in the ruins of Panamint City offers some unauthenticated Scottiana. Its title is *The Monte Cristo of Death Valley,* but as the front pages are missing from this sole damaged copy I do not know by whom it was written or published. The author describes a remote camp of Scotty's "equipped with pieces of furniture not to be found in many city homes." The magnitude and heft of a bathtub and "large easy rocker" made him wonder how they were brought over the steep trails. He notes that among the provisions was everything the "most fastidious persons" could require, "among them nicknacks such as after-dinner mints," adding that two notices adorned the premises, to wit:

> *"Eat all you want, stay as long as*
> *you want, but don't take anything away.*
> *Look out for the pet rattlesnake. Don't*
> *kill her. She won't bite you.*
> —*Walter Scott"*

"Another thing that made the boys laugh," writes this historian, "was a large array of solid silver spoons that he had as souvenirs. They were laid side by side. There was one from each of the leading railroads and hotels—the Southern Pacific, Santa Fe, Salt Lake, Erie, Burlington, besides a great many of the leading hotels throughout the country—one from each of them."

Scotty's sense of humor is laid on with a certain heavy-handed gusto. The chief purpose of his escapades seems to be getting himself talked about; the target of his stories, the same. Publicity is the measuring stick of his pleasure. And if he can make the other fellow foolish, so much the better. He'll go to a lot of trouble to accomplish that.

"An editor of the Los Angeles *Times* asked me to lunch. An editor or a manager or something. A big shot. Y'understand?" I said I did. The picture conveyed was of an impressive office and one of those double-breasted personalities.

"Stuffy. Get it? Well, we waited around a bit. He'd corralled a couple of other guests. Easterners. When we started down the elevator I said I was sorry but I was broke and didn't have a cent so I couldn't buy the lunch. They laughed at that.

"Out on the sidewalk I said something more about being broke. I think they were a bit embarrassed. Expected a touch

118

or something. Y'understand? Well, at the corner a ragged-looking character was standing. Gray-haired and seedy.

"I went over to that bum. The editor and his guests could see and hear me all right.

"'Bo,' I said. 'I'm broke. Can you lend me enough to eat on?'

"'Sure,' he said. 'You're welcome to what I got.'

"So he fished down in his old blue levis and pulled out four one-thousand-dollar bills. He gave me two of 'em.

"I said, 'Thank you,' and went along with the others. They seemed sorta silent and surprised.

"Pretty soon one of them asked me who my friend was.

"'Him?' I said. 'I dunno. Never seen him before.'

"'Was that two thousand dollars he gave you?' another asked.

"I said it was. 'He knows who I am,' I said. 'He knows some day he'll get it back.'

"'Well, I'll be damned!' said one of the men. He was from New York.

"'Now,' I said, 'I can pay for the lunch.' But they wouldn't let me."

Scotty pushed the sombrero back and ruffled his hand through the thatch of fluffy white hair that looks sometimes as if desert mice had slept in it.

"Y'understand?" His blue eyes twinkled.

I said I thought I did.

"Yeah," he spat decisively. "That hobo was Johnson."

I imagine Albert Johnson got as much fun out of it as Scotty did.

In 1928 Scotty published in a Nevada paper this notice:
"Will all my friends and enemies keep away from the shack

until it is done? Then Johnson and myself will stand on our heads and wait on you."

At the time he estimated the shack would be completed "forty years from today." So there is still time for the swimming pool, the moat, gardens, and other appurtenances to be finished on schedule.

In the meantime those who are not as kindly disposed as they might be to this Barnum-Munchausen team, should remember that the partnership has never tried to sell anything to the public. There has been no promoting for profit. Promoting for publicity, no doubt, but that hurt no one. And no one, unless he wants to, is obliged to visit the Castle, or meet Scotty or Johnson—or even read about them! Although all three are well worth seeing.

As to the true story, about either the Castle, Scotty, or Johnson, I'm sure I don't know. I've said before I wished Johnson would write it. But I doubt whether even he could be a veracious Boswell to Walter Scott. As a matter of fact, I don't believe Scott could be that himself.

Once a newspaperman went to the Castle.

"Scotty," he said, "Mr. Hearst has told me to write your straight story. From the beginning to date. No matter how long it takes, I'm to dig up the facts."

"Okay," said Scotty. "I'll help you. Don't just get the stuff from me. You go to these people who know me. Get the dope from them and then come back."

Scotty gave his visitor half a dozen names. They were men of Reno, Las Vegas, San Francisco, Los Angeles, Chicago.

Weeks later the writer returned.

"See 'em all?" Scotty asked.

The writer nodded. "Every one of them. They all talked, too. Very cooperative."

120

"That's fine," said Scotty. "Between 'em they know all about me."

"The trouble is," the reporter went on, "each one told me an altogether different story."

Which is the way it is. And, I think, likely evermore shall be.

As to Albert Johnson, his friends say at heart he is a hoaxer who has extracted value received in vicarious amusement for all he has spent. The whole modern fable, according to one school of thought, can be set down as a monstrous practical joke on the public. And the suckers have had a good show in return for their applause, which is all it has cost them.

There is a legend that Albert Johnson came to the desert in bad health, his days numbered. The yarn has pathos, and I have a notion even Scotty has used it now and then. But the tale is not true. That I have on the authority of a letter from the Johnson office itself. I wrote asking him for the facts. Johnson, so the reply said, "not being available," his secretary stated that "there is no substance for the statement that Mr. Johnson recovered his health in Death Valley."

Apparently Albert Johnson was hale and hearty when he came West with Scotty. There the sunshine, outdoor living, and his jester have kept him that way. I suspect Johnson's implication, if he got around to talking about such things as the measure of the return his desert adventurings has given him for the cash they've cost, would be a question: Is any price too high to pay for health and contentment and laughter?

It is not hard to understand the affection Albert Johnson holds for Death Valley and the partner it brought him.

13. Trilobites and Tarantulas

*I*F you'd taken out a fishing license in Death Valley five hundred million years ago your catch would have been trilobites. And if there had been an open season for hunters a few million years later, Ice Age elk and bison and titanotheriums could have been your game.

Such were the forerunners of the wild life of today. Everything about the Valley has its foundations deep in the past. The reason for the country's appearance, its climate, and its wealth all stem from ancient geological activities, and its zoology developed along with its topography.

White men came to the Valley proper only one short century ago. Indians were there perhaps a thousand years earlier. Animal life was present half a billion years or so before the Indians.

In the vast span of the intervening eons, the wild game has changed its pattern to fit the cloth of environment, drastic alteration likely occurring mostly during the last fifty thousand years, along with the increasing aridity. From the process of survival and adaptation have emerged the desert denizens we now know, conditioned to heat, drought, and sparse forage.

Before we establish a nodding acquaintance with the more common beasts and birds of today, it is entertaining to consider their ancestors of yesterday. As it happens, those same articulate rocks which tell the story of the Valley's creation, also recorded much about the ancient fauna, resident and transient.

The first living things in the area where Death Valley now is dwelt under water. The fossils found in the limestones of the Paleozoic era are the who's who of that early marine life, its dominant member a crablike creature called a trilobite. Emerging from the era of algae and single-celled organisms, the trilobites were the first citizens of their day, wee creatures often measuring as much as three inches in length.

From the era when Death Valley was wet and its animals lived in water, there developed some of the more primitive reptiles as well as amphibians, who found their livelihood on land as well as in the water.

Next, as we riffle through the pages of our tabloid natural history, we come upon the Mesozoic era, say two hundred million years ago, with its dinosaurs and their curious brethren, who grazed chiefly upon tree ferns. Thence forward through the Cenozoic times when mammals developed in great variety, from the massive titanotheriums, a forebear of the modern rhinoceros, to a small three-toed horse. From these emerged, as more millions of years rolled away, fauna with familiar names—horses of several kinds, camels, antelopes, members of the cat family, and various wading birds. The tracks of all of them have been preserved, and the bones of some have been found.

Finally, animal life, somewhat as we now know it, became resident in the region after the glacial period, perhaps a paltry dozen thousand years ago. And as the climate changed, the requirements of survival changed the animals, too. Quite some centuries before Columbus went voyaging the four-footed and winged citizens of Death Valley looked and acted just about as they do today, where man has left them alone.

The ancient trilobites are gone, but fish still flourish in this hottest and driest of all valleys. Salt fish at that.

These, if you please, are "desert sardines," a top-minnow with a name longer than his body, *Cyprinodon salinus.* Some carnivorous water beetles, wading birds, and even coyotes feed on them, and Indians found them palatable before the era of tin cans set in.

The Panamint Indians are described as using the species for food by gathering quantities in large porous baskets, aided by brooms made of tules, the reed that grows in damp places. The contents were then baked, with the fish lying between layers of tule reeds and these alternating with layers of hot ashes. This practice has apparently been discontinued for two or more generations.

Once ancestors of these tiny fish lived in ancient Lake Manly. As the lake evaporated they retreated to the small salt ponds of the Valley's southern floor, and to the rivulets that are the final termini of the Amargosa River, where they evolved into different species. When the rare rains come these rivulets enlarge to shallow streams, thereafter shrinking again and leaving their small fry stranded on the saltbeds, there either to dehydrate into nothingness or provide an *hors d'oeuvre* for some coyote's dinner.

A relish, too, for the questing scientist. For these diminutive fish are impressive evidence to substantiate theories about the changing physical geography of the region they inhabited for a good many thousand years, and where they now live as close neighbors to their fossilized ancestors.

Briefly, their presence in widely separated waters shows

that once what is now Death Valley was long ago the heart of a drainage system that included Owens Valley, Searles Basin, Panamint Valley, Pahrump Valley, and the Mojave River Basin, as well as the Amargosa Valley which still drains into it.*

If you will look at the map, or see the country from any of its high vantage points, you realize that today each of the valleys named above is separated from the others—and from Death Valley—by massive mountain ranges. But in geological yesterdays, where Death Valley is now was the final sump, Lake Manly, connected with all of them by waterways navigable at least for little fish.

In each locality the minnows have developed differently. Environment and evolution saw to that.

Robert R. Miller of the University of Michigan has written learnedly about these surviving symbols of the past:

The distribution of the fishes of the Death Valley System substantiates the physiographic evidence for the former hydrographic continuity of these basins. The occurrence of the minnow genus *Siphateles* in the Owens and Mojave rivers, of *Cyprinodon* in the Amargosa–Death Valley region and Owens Valley, and of the cyprinodont, *Empetrichthys*, in Pahrump Valley and in Ash Meadows of the Amargosa drainage, testifies to a former connection of the waters of these basins. Local differentiation in each of the three genera suggests that the basins have been isolated since the Pleistocene.

One of the most strongly marked of the isolated fish is our little friend the *Cyprinodon salinus* found by the thousand in Salt Creek. And, if you please, a *new* species tagged with his new name as recently as 1943, although quietly going about his business of evoluting since the Pleistocene age when

* See Chapter 7, "Geologic Yesterdays."

he was cut off from his fellows by the mountains that rose between their several habitats.

Had not Park Naturalist E. A. Alberts shown me Dr. Miller's paper, this book, like all its predecessors, would have miscalled Death Valley's one and only fish *macularius,* which would have been grievously inaccurate.

Because the limited mammal life of Death Valley is mostly nocturnal, birds are particularly noticeable in daylight hours. Approximately one hundred and seventy species have been recorded below sea level. Most of them are migrants or winter visitors, and include a surprisingly large number of water birds, but fourteen species make the valley floor their permanent home. The big black desert raven is perhaps the most commonly noted.

More than twenty years ago, Dr. Joseph Grinnell issued a report on some comparatively brief investigations he had made in 1917 and 1920. That first listing for the California Academy of Sciences included one hundred and twenty-four species. Dr. Grinnell noted that the environment was "most prolific of bird life. . . . The mesquite," he wrote, "harbors an abundance of insects, the foliage and beans are edible for some birds, and it affords shade and protective cover." Much of the floor of the Valley, its sparse vegetation mostly the mesquite bush, is indeed an admirable sanctuary for certain birds.

Ducks and geese are frequently Valley visitors, more in evidence during the southward migrations of early autumn than when going north in spring. Even in coolish weather these travelers have difficulty in finding water to light on in this essentially waterless region.

A report written in 1875 by Lieutenant Birnie records a hazard the migrant birds encountered even in pioneer times.

The highest part of the Funeral range is a resort for Indians, who gather the pine nuts in the fall. Here was also observed the peculiar blinds made by the Indians just beside the springs for killing the birds that come in numbers to the only water to be had. These blinds have the general appearance of a beehive, are made of rushes and small boughs interlaced, with an opening for entrance on the side away from the spring. The interior is large enough to seat one person, a small opening being toward the water through which to shoot the arrow with a string attached for recovering it, so no alarm is produced.

Beside the machinations of man, the climate of Death Valley provides its own peculiar difficulties for some forms of wild life. Rising from the torrid sink in the later summer months is a vast funnel of super-heated air. That funnel boils skyward many thousand feet, often with great velocity. Ducks frequently are caught and overcome by this seering maelstrom. There are numerous authenticated instances where birds—usually teal and mallard—fall to the ground exhausted, to die on the dry sands or on the broiling oiled roads.

Eagles, scourge of mountain lambs and all little people of the sandy wastes, are mostly in the highlands. All the Monument is hunting ground for hawks. The road-runners, crested, long-legged and long-tailed, rush along highway or sand with equal intentness, seeming always to be going somewhere in a hurry. He is said sometimes to do battle, and successfully, with small rattlesnakes.

Beside the road-runner, the resident birds who stay on after the easy times of early spring are over, include the raven, Gambel's quail, the verdin, and Say's phoebe, all true citizens of the desert able to thrive for long periods without water. The minimum moisture needed they find in the leaves of succulent plants, berries, insects, and the bodies of dead lizards, rabbits, and rodents, depending upon the individual diet.

Of these year-round residents, Say's phoebe contributes most in liveliness and certainly in music, to the pattern of life in the Valley. This phoebe is a flycatcher of gray-brown color, the undersides rusty. Before dawn he sings persistently his plaintive reveille. With daylight, there is less song, for he is busy flashing in swift sorties as he captures his flying breakfast. Then more song, until midday heat sends him to shaded refuge beneath bushes or rock ledges.

If it is a dry year and the feed meager, the bird migrants simply remain in the Valley for shorter visits and move on to greener pastures. But the native nesting birds have no choice but to tighten their belts and survive the hard times as best they may.

For one thing, in the bad seasons, they cut down their families. With fewer mouths to feed food goes farther.

That desert birds under such conditions do actually practice birth control is attested by that experienced naturalist, Edmund C. Jaeger. In his handbook, *The California Desert*, he writes:

It is a fact well worth noting that during the drought years when there is little promise of food supplies many of the desert birds, such as the insect-eating cactus wren and the thrashers, full of avian wisdom, nest early, or cut down the number of eggs, or forego both nest and egg-laying, passing over the season without offspring.

In times when such domestic forbearance does not distract from the joys of living, the birds seem to relish their odd environment. The killdeer wades the briny pools in search of bugs and beetles. Rock wrens go about their business from sea level to the tip of Telescope Peak, Gambel's quail scurry about Furnace Creek Ranch, and mountain doves reside wherever water may be. Warblers, flycatchers, sparrows, bluebirds, robins, and mocking birds are winter visitors, and meadow larks sing lustily in the spring.

The yucca, or so-called Spanish Bayonet, in its blooming season is a lovely thing and you'll see it in profusion along the approaches to Death Valley, but in the Monument itself there are few outside the Grapevine Mountain area. The yucca's spears, sharp and strong, make it a fortress for its friends, and a menace to the unwanted, which the birds know well.

I have found feathers near yuccas and wondered why, until one day I saw a hawk chasing a linnet. The linnet flew straight for the nearest yucca and dove into its protective thicket. The hawk swooped close, then flew away. The yucca was like a city of refuge, its spears far enough apart for the body of a small bird to enter, too close together for a larger one to follow. The same sort of emergency shelter is provided for birds and tiny beasts by several kinds of cactus and thorny growths.

That day, too, I solved the mystery of feathers seen on the sand beside a yucca. A little bird was fluttering, obviously in distress, and when I approached I saw what had happened. In his fright he had flown blindly and struck a spear, impaling himself. As gently as possible I released the little fellow and soon, after a brief period of bewildered convalescence, he flew away.

There, if you will, is another house-that-Jack-built parable in reverse, stemming from nature's system of balances. Fewer yuccas and cacti, fewer small birds and beasts, the shrinkage of each in turn disturbing other balances farther along the scale.

There are two kinds of rattlesnakes in the Death Valley country, neither of them numerous—Panamint rattler and the "sidewinder." On the higher levels the snakes are large, three feet long and over, and as thick as a man's wrist. They are more sluggish in movement than the smaller snakes, but probably more deadly, with their larger sac of poison.

In the Valley, the sidewinders are so called because of their peculiar gait. Instead of the snakelike, serpentine motion of the big mountain variety, the sidewinders throw themselves from side to side. Coming toward you, they look as if they were going away. The sidewinder is much smaller than his highland relative, averaging from eighteen to twenty-eight inches in length, and about as large around as a man's thumb. They make a trail on the sand of parallel cross bars, while the mountain rattlers leave a serpentine trail.

Both species of rattlesnake carry a sac of venom behind their jaws, to which is attached a pair of hypodermic needles. Actually, a rattlesnake is a very fair reptile, for he gives warning to any who may encroach upon his domain and there is no sound out-of-doors so unmistakable—and alarming—as the tocsin of that rattle. Like most wild animals under normal conditions, given a chance, a snake will move out of your way.

While rattlesnakes in the usual routine of their Death Valley living seem to thrive, apparently they succumb easily to unusual treatment. In July, 1940, Ranger Houston carried one from Emigrant Ranger Station to Furnace Creek in a burlap bag soaked with water, the thermometer being above 120°, and the snake died during the hour's journey. I have read that a rattlesnake cannot survive the direct sun rays of a summer in Death Valley. Perhaps this has been established as a fact, but I have still to find anyone who has seen a snake die of sunstroke. Anyway, there is no record of any test being made. Which now is not true of scorpions.

Ted Ogston, Chief Ranger, found a scorpion five inches long beneath a trashbasket in his home one day in August,

1945, when the outside temperature as shown by the weather bureau thermometer was 118° in the shade.

Right there Ogston decided what he didn't know about rattlesnakes he would find out about scorpions. He took the animal out on the stone patio. From the first direct touch of the sun's rays it was apparent the scorpion was unhappy. He immediately did his best to reach a shady spot, but each time was pushed back. Meanwhile Ogston with his wristwatch kept time. Within two minutes the animal started to quiver. Then it exuded a white substance from its mandible. Some seconds later the scorpion was rigidly stiff and three minutes from the start of the heat treatment he was dead.

Ogston doubts that a rattler would be as susceptible. But it may well be that a snake with absolutely no shade could not survive direct sun temperatures that probably exceed 150°.

In the Monument there are centipedes and tarantulas, whose looks are worse than their bites. There seems to be no record of serious effect from the sting of either. An odd fact about these desert tarantulas—they are black hairy spiders often as large as the palm of one's hand—has been noted by Park personnel. October seems to be moving time for the local tribe, when they all start going *somewhere*. Just where, or why is not known. During that month they often are encountered crossing the oiled roads. In at least one season the general route seemed to be northward.

14. Mountain Sheep aud Burros

*W*HILE the habits of most of Death Valley's four-footed citizens are nocturnal, exceptions are coyotes, occasional bobcats, and the ubiquitous antelope ground squirrel with his bushy tail curved over his back, scuttling about everywhere without regard to altitude, environment, or daylight.

And, of course, the Monument's most exclusive resident, the mountain sheep, whose ancestors were emigrants from Asia who came across the ice of the Bering Straits, their forebears Marco Polo sheep. The variety known as Nelson Death Valley sheep, *Ovis nelsoni,* are a modified version of the bighorns of the Rockies.

Once these desert sheep periodically crossed the intervening valleys to the Sierra but there has been no record of such summer vacationing for many years. In all the ranges of eastern and southeastern California there are today perhaps thirty-five hundred mountain sheep of whom Superintendent Goodwin estimates about five hundred are within the Monument and its immediate neighborhood, a number said to be gradually increasing.

The rams, alone of all American wild animals, have circling horns. The ewes have straight horns. A large ram will weigh between one hundred and fifty and two hundred pounds. The circumference of his broad tapering horn at its base is about fifteen inches and its length along the outside curve in the neighborhood of forty inches, with a widest spread of around twenty-one inches. The coloring of mountain sheep varies from pale gray or brown to dirty white, the rump, hams, and belly being white. Sierra dwellers are lighter in tone than their desert relatives. Wild sheep are not covered with wool but with hide and hair similar to a mule deer's, their eyes are yellow and amazingly keen, though their hearing is very poor, because their small ears seem to be infested with ticks.

Bold climbers, these sheep can go anywhere and at amazing speed, their endurance equaling their agility. Nature has shod them with skill. The hoofs are long, narrow, cupped with sharp edges and with a sort of rubber lining near the heel that has the virtues of a concentrated skid-proof tire.

In dry times sheep need to drink perhaps not oftener than twice or even once a week. They supplement their water supply with moisture from the grizzly cactus which grows at high altitudes, and from certain roots which may be those of the Matilija poppy. A reason their horns often are battered and blunted is that they are used to dig up such roots from the rocky ground as well as to pulverize stalks to get at the moisture.

The sheep's worst enemies are golden eagles and man. Now, thanks to the National Park Service, abetted by California and Nevada conservation policies, man has protected the vanishing species from man, so that the magnificent animals will be perpetuated.

After the grasses and flowers of their brief green-growing season have been burnished off by summer suns, the sheep

133

take to the mountains and stay there. And the highlands around Death Valley are high indeed, remote ferocious places without cover or trails or water, ideal in many ways for the survival of these canniest and most truly wild of all American mammals.

However, up in Grapevine Canyon you may get the impression that mountain sheep are pretty commonplace fellows. On a fence of his lower 'Vine ranch, Death Valley Scotty has posted a sign which reads:

These Sheep are Tame
Don't Shoot Them

On occasion this good teller of tales will admit there is quite a band of *Ovis nelsoni* that practically eats out of his hand, but they haven't been seen by others.

Actually, the likelihood of your encountering sheep in Death Valley is not rosy unless you spend much time at the higher altitudes. There is, for instance, Helen Ogston, wife of the Chief Ranger, who has lived in the Monument for seven years and traveled much about it. In those seven years she has seen seven sheep, and that was all at one time when she was climbing Telescope Peak.

"But," she will add, which is encouraging to the casual visitor, "within the last few months I've known several people who were in the Valley just one day and saw sheep. One ram was right down close to Furnace Creek Ranch!"

There is one more large quadruped in the Monument you probably will encounter. He is a sizable fearless fellow with an imponderable disposition who operates both by day and night, has mastered all the devices of survival, and, because of familiarity, is no respecter of man.

Although "exotic" doesn't seem exactly the right word for a burro, that is what these beasts are, a species not indigenous to the country.

These Death Valley burros, who at their peak numbered an estimated twenty-five hundred are descendants of animals escaped from prospectors or let loose in the desert. They in turn were lineal descendants of the asses introduced by the Spaniards, those compact little carriers who bore their burdens for the padres who first found California.

Seemingly, burros have outlived their usefulness in the current scheme of things. Changing times have changed styles of desert travel. Today roads of some sort lead almost everywhere and the modern prospector gets about in his jaloppy. Gasoline is easier to carry than hay, cars are quicker, and they stay where you park them, which burros don't do. When ore is packed out of remote claims, mules are more efficient than burros and cost less in trouble and money.

But at that, the sleek and cheerful burro is an ornament to the desert countryside. Nothing four-footed is more picturesque. Especially alluring are the toylike youngsters with their long ears, shaggy pelts thick as teddy-bears, and coltish charms.

The burro prospers under the direst conditions, multiplies amazingly, and consumes the fodder the wild animals must have, as well as polluting springs and grazing grounds so that mountain sheep will have none of them. Also, of course, he destroys anything he can get at which man plants. And as no means ever has been devised to keep a burro from getting where he wants to get, the scourge is a real one on all counts.

So, regretfully—because their philosophy is to permit no killing in a National Park or Monument—the authorities from time to time indulge in official burro hunting, though no private sportsman may take a hand. Thus the harmful population is kept within bounds and the Park Service maintains the balance of nature, keystone of its administration of the primitive heritages it holds in trust for the public.

A burro hunt can be something special. There are few game animals which require more exertion, patience, and skill to bag than members of the remote wild bands in the back countries of the Monument. For all-around craftiness, you can't beat an experienced burro who has been hunted. His ancestry and his familiarity with man make him that way. Any animal who can prosper where he does has his wits about him.

Burros know when a man has a gun and when he hasn't, and act accordingly. They also can calculate the effective range of a rifle. Beyond that range they eye you with mild interest. Within that range—but you don't get that close if they see you first, which they usually do.

Famous among Death Valley's wilder burros was one with a bell about his neck fastened with a wire that could not be broken, for a leather strap would have been chewed off by his brothers. That belled burro had been some prospector's pack animal who'd wandered away from his responsibilities. In the silent desert air you could hear the bell a very long way. That is, if the animal moved his head. But once the hunt was on the bell-carrier knew better. He'd stand absolutely still, even when he was far beyond rifle range.

Of course, there were stories about that burro. There are stories about everything in Death Valley. Next to borax the region yields more fables than anything else, for it boasts other notable specialists in tall tales beside Death Valley Scotty.

"The other animals," I was assured by my Ranger friend who excelled at this specialized hunting, "would bring grass up to that burro so he could eat without moving about and
136

make any noise with the bell. I watched him once with glasses when he stood beside a rock he'd picked out because it was almost exactly the color of his hide. He never moved his head more than enough to lean over and lap up the tufts of grass his pals put on the rock. Then they'd stand around looking as if they were laughing at us humans. I was too far away to hear their burro talk."

Myself, I never saw that burro with the bell.

Although mountain sheep, burros, and a few other authentic desert animals do not confine their activities to the night, essentially the wild life of such a region as Death Valley is nocturnal.

This night life shuns attention. It is almost soundless. Unless for the chance illumination of an automobile headlight or hand-flash—or the skillfully placed photographer's flare—you are apt to sense very little of this teeming world of desert darkness.

Throughout the sandy wastes that in sunshine may seem so devoid of life, once night has come, birds and beasts and reptiles crawl and run and fly. But not until dusk do they bestir themselves. The bright hot days they sleep away in burrows and dark crevices among the rocks.

And when the next dawn comes the story of the bustling night has been written in tracks upon the sand, its paragraphs, for those with the knowledge and the patience to read them, punctuated with the skeletons and scattered feathers of tragedy.

William Beebe has written of the delightful wonders of minute areas of jungle. For him, an acre or a square yard can hold as great interest in the diversity of the tales it has to tell, as a naturalist could come upon in any farflung expedition. It need be neither miles nor magnitude that contributes most of the seldom-seen worlds of wild life.

In his book *Jungle Peace,* Will has written: "The tropical jungle by day is the most wonderful place in the world. At night I am sure it is the most weirdly beautiful of all places outside the world. For it is primarily unearthly, unreal."

In its different way the desert is as wonderful. A well-selected scrap of desert would yield not one thousandth of the living organisms Beebe found in his British Guiana square yard, but, I think, as much of exciting beauty. Perhaps he will come one day and give us *Desert Peace.*

In the sand is the matrix that records what the humble tiny people are up to each night when you may not see them. The story is set down precisely on pages which the breezes erase clean by day, ready to receive fresh confidences in the new night.

On the firm surfaces are winding trails, minute lacelike scrolls, the sterner footprints of larger predators. In their own shorthand the people of the night have written their stories. There are many authors and many separate tales. They are of home-building, love, industry, the chase, battle, escape, death. The notes are set down each in its own special characters, by tiny beetles, snakes, rodents, chipmunks, desert fox, coyotes, badgers, spiders, ant-lions, vinageroons, rabbits, lizards, mice, and a score of infinitesimal gremlins whose penmanship is very faint indeed. In contrast to these last, the final entries are bold, made with the arrival of dawn, by road-runners, quail, and decisive hawks, all swift death for the wee ones who loitered too long beyond the security of their daylight homes.

Of an early morning consult any strip of sand near your hotel, camp, or sleeping bag, especially where there is some shelter from mesquite or other desert growth, and you find intimate notes inscribed in the night for you to decipher.

138

If you have any affection at all for little wild things, perhaps no other open sesame to the lure of the desert can be so potent as this retrospective glimpse, mirrored in its sands, of the unseen life of its small citizens.

15. Little People of the Desert

IN individual size the roster of wild life in Death Valley Monument contrasts poorly with wilderness or jungle regions. The desert is a place of little people. But for all their insignificance compared to such as lion, elk, and elephant, the desert dwellers are every bit as interesting, and far more approachable.

Among the diminutive animals for whom the Monument is home are white-footed mice, kangaroo rats and pocket mice. All of them are friendly, vivid creatures, devoid of the traits which make household rats and mice disliked.

George McClellan Bradt has written delightfully of this trio. Remarkable is his observation about a pet pocket mouse (Genus *Perognathus*): "Canary bird seed was his nightly fare. All other food he scorned. He even refused water. Never during his entire captivity [eight months] did he have a drink. Yet on the summer evening that we freed him he was as healthy and as sleek as when first caught. The desert is dry, but not half so dry as a pocket mouse."

A kangaroo rat (Genus *Dipodmys*) likewise went four

months without a drink of water, although lettuce in its artificial menu probably provided needed moisture. Commenting
on this lesser kangaroo's arid nature, William T. Hornaday in
his *American Natural History,* calls them "both fireproof and
waterproof, for no amount of heat affects them and the absence of water does not seem to depress their spirits."

This quaint beast is a desert edition of a kangaroo in miniature, with disproportionately long hind legs, large feet, and
lengthy tufted tail. It travels with long and high kangaroo-
like jumps, its tail a rudder of sorts, its short forelegs seldom
touching the ground.

There is a small population of badgers—estimated at one
hundred and fifty within the Monument—and found from
sea level to about seven thousand feet, and two varieties of
pygmy skunk, one with broad, the other with narrow stripes.
The desert kitfox is a sprightly being, a smaller and even more
delicate edition of the swift, about thirty-two inches long and
paler in its tones of gray and brown. The desert kitfox has in-
satiable curiosity and mischievous habits. One of its quirks
is to cut the laces in shoes left beside a camper's bed.

Jackrabbits and cottontail rabbits are fairly plentiful in some
parts of the Monument, though there is no abundance of them.
Nature's balance seems to keep down this population which
in some places becomes a plague, though of late the number
of rabbits in the Valley is on the increase. A natural con-
comitant of that improving larder has been a similar increase
in bobcats and coyotes.

Characteristic of these deserts is the chuckwalla, an outsize
lizard of fearsome appearance—he has the contours and coloring of a fabulous monster in miniature—and entire harmless-
ness, a mild desert vegetarian who feeds on buds and leaves
and is the largest fellow of his kind in the United States.

His only defensive weapons are his protective coloration

141

and his habit of inflating himself once he is well tucked into some crack beneath rocks so that he wedges himself against the walls of his retreat and it is impossible to pull him out. This apparently works well against foxes, coyotes, eagles, and hawks, but not against Indians. With a sharp stick they puncture the puffed-up 'walla's hide so that he flattens out like a deflated balloon and is dragged forth easily.

A good sized chuckwalla may measure as much as two feet from head to tailtip, though mostly they are slightly smaller. Their conformation is that of a typical lizard, with dragon-like head, loose skin that has the look of rather scabrous armor, and a blunt clumsy tail. The tail may be orange with dull black bands, or marked with soiled white.

The activities of this pint-sized vegetarian descendant of the ancient dinosaur vary pretty well in proportion to the sunshine. In the winter he hibernates and even when in circulation again chill days slow down his activity. In the hottest weather, when he is full of scamper, a chuckwalla becomes immobile at any suspicion of danger, his coloring blending cunningly with the landscape, so that he looks like just another mottled rock.

Doubtless chuckwallas were an important item in the diet of the ancient Indians and as early as 1849 they figured in the menus of white pioneers. J. B. Colton, a member of one of the original parties of gold-seekers, wrote: "Sometimes we found a big lizard or chuckwalla and sometimes a little desert turtle, and we ate up all the snakes and ravens we could catch." Which were probably very few.

In his journal of April 28, 1866, a Valley visitor made this slightly contradictory entry: "Game there is none. A few does found their way to the springs only to find their way to our kettles. Some of us tried roast lizard by way of variation. Most say they are equal to any frog that was ever cooked."

142

Indians mostly ate the chuckwalla raw. Probably the only cleaning indulged in was to dust the sand off. While I have not eaten this local lizard, I have sampled others like him in Central America and found the meat compact, sweetish, and sometimes reasonably tender. Parboiling before baking seems to have been recommended.

The vinegaroon—sometimes called a sun-spider or whip-scorpion—is a resident with the appearance of a giant spider, pinkish cream in color and very swift, his usual length about two inches, two feelers in front perpetually weaving as he moves forward. When disturbed he emits an odor like vinegar, whence his most-used name. This unattractive character, who is like something conjured up in a very bad dream is harmless, so far as humans are concerned, since he carries no venom.

A Death Valley facsimile of a mongoose-and-cobra battle can be staged between a vinegaroon and a scorpion. Put the two in a small enclosure and they go at each other with no holds barred, the scorpion squat, tenacious, the vinegaroon a dancing, swirling tuft of fury. Apparently the scorpion is always the winner. And there's nothing left of the looser for every bit of him is eaten by the scorpion, so that at least the battlefield remains tidy.

Hundreds of species of insects live in the area, supplying birds and lizards with food. Except for the inch-long horsefly which draws blood when it bites (encountered only in hot weather), most of the insects are very unobtrusive. Butterflies, some of rare beauty, appear in the spring when the flowers bloom, and at other times masses of butterflies move across the Valley in colorful clouds, usually traveling from east to west, their origin and destination unknown. In the evening bats circle and swoop, feeding luxuriously on flying insects;

143

in the daytime they sleep in caves or in abandoned mine tunnels.

The bats adapt themselves quickly to the conveniences provided by their human fellow citizens. Beside a number of the houses where the Park personnel live are little pools, which the bats take over at dusk. They zoom down, hit the surface lightly with a little splash easily heard, gather in a mouthful, and take off for a refreshing round of the darkling evening sky before they come in for another drink.

A horned toad is as ornery a looking reptile as one is apt to imagine, with a crown of horns on his head, sharp-pointed scales studding back and sides, and rows of spines running around his broad flattened body and thick blunt tail. He has a wide determined mouth and a high forehead which give him, head-on, a certain intellectual though repellent appearance.

Beneath a horned toad's bizarre exterior beats a friendly heart and a harmless nature. Scratch one under the throat and he'll stick out his chins—he has as many as a dowager— roll his little eyes in ecstasy and all but purr.

With their prominent tails, scales on the body, five-clawed toes on each foot, and other anatomical features, horned toads are definitely lizards. They belong to the family *Iguanidae* and the genus *Phrynosoma*. Their color, usually light gray, varies according to their environment. In regions of black lava rocks their skin is generally dark, while in the mountain country the markings may be red or even bluish. Their coloration protects them from their natural enemies, birds and snakes.

The horned lizard's spiny exterior makes him an unappetizing meal for desert animals. The side-winder has been known to attack the horned lizard and swallow it. Weldon Woodson

144

has recorded in *Desert Magazine* * that the results are often disastrous. The lizard, still alive within the snake's body, will turn its head from side to side, gouging its horns through the lining wall of the reptile, until victor and vanquish die together. Mr. Woodson writes:

At sunset, the horned lizard pokes its nose in the sand, wags its head from side to side, and pushes with its feet until the fore part of its body is covered. Then it wiggles its tail as it bores in and gradually disappears beneath the surface. It remains under cover until late the next morning when the warm sun's rays bring it back to the surface again.

Certain horned lizards possess a pearly translucent scale near the center of the head, which according to some theories, is the remnant of a third eye. It is believed that remote ancestors of this reptile actually made use of three eyes, but the middle one, because of disuse and other factors, ceased to function. Even so, when the lizard buries itself in the sand it arranges to have this peculiar scale close to the surface. Science suggests the possibility that the vestigial third eye can distinguish between light and dark. There is the possibility that the sun's rays as they reach it through the thin layer of sand rouse the lizard from its siesta.

Desert tortoise are occasionally encountered. They are harmless creatures measuring eight to ten inches across their shells which seem rather more rounded and less oblong than are wet-country turtles. These plodding introverts go about their business like tiny tanks, seemingly with more persistence than sense. The tortoise butts at any obstacle in his path and keeps butting until he overcomes it or admits himself permanently stymied, rather than submit to an intellectual compromise like finding a way round.

* A periodical brimming with delightful desert lore and fine photographs, recommended to anyone interested in our American deserts, their people, animals, plants, places, and past. Address: El Centro, California.

The clown of the Valley's tricksy wild people is the neotoma, that being the formal name for a pack- or woodrat, encountered frequently around all desert resting places.

Neotoma is a kleptomaniac with a conscience. For while he will pack off anything that is movable, he always leaves something in its place. This habit is responsible for his third name, trade rat. There is still a fourth designation, and a big one, for this little fellow; the Hopi Indians called him *Kee-hua-cahl-a*.

By whatever name, the packrat is not directly related to the house rat and, indeed, won't stay around after these disagreeable European immigrants move in.

The packrat has the face of a gentle rabbit, large black eyes, and batlike ears. Its soft slate-gray fur resembles that of the Andean chinchilla. Unlike the house rat, it has a hairy tail and white feet and underparts. In arid regions it usually lives in large nests of coarse sticks built about the base of a spiny cholla. In the mountains it resides in crevices and small caves, the entrances protected by masses of cactus lobes and pads.

The neotoma is a rodent. It has two large incisor teeth in each jaw, separated by an empty space from the molar teeth, as have the squirrel, marmot, and beaver. He does his packing in those pouches, sometimes stuffed so full the serious little face seems afflicted with a bad case of mumps.

The neotoma is attracted to bright shiny objects and sometimes in his nest is found an odd assortment of whatever has struck his fancy and is transportable, from buttons and bits of glass to gold nuggets. Packrats' taste in trinkets is unpredictable, nor are they respecters of personages. T. R. Goodwin, superintendent of the Monument, is a miniature railroad addict and has a shed back of his home housing an elaborate display of pint-sized railroading, complete with electric locomotives and trains, signals and switches that work, a village, railroad yards, trucks, and people. One day he found that every tiny tree and human figure had disappeared. The work of some eccentric vandal, he thought. It was that, all right. A few mornings later the trees and figures were back approximately where they had been, but spilled about horizontally instead of in verticle orderliness. One should not expect too much from a packrat.

Back in 1889, packrats figured in early Death Valley tribulations. That winter C. B. Zabriskie of the Pacific Coast Borax Company, which had just bought Furnace Creek Ranch, planned to feed his horses on one hundred and eighty sacks of grain that were stored at the Ranch.

But when he got there the cupboard was bare.

Zabriskie asked Jim Dayton, the caretaker, to show him the sacked grain.

"I can show you the one hundred and eighty sacks, but there ain't no grain."

"What have you done with it?"

"Nothing. But the packrats have."

Going to the warehouse Zabriskie found the one hundred and eighty bags with every kernel of grain packed away. Alongside the empty sacks was a pile of sticks, stone and all sorts of odds and ends the rats had left in exchange for the grain.

That time the horses went hungry and there was no enthusiasm for the quaint tricks of packrattery. The story, by the way, is quite true.

A more imaginative yarn, not untypical of the Valley, concerns a tame packrat who was trained ever so carefully to collect from their rightful owners negotiable items regarded highly by his master, like nuggets and silver dollars. The system worked well for some time until an attack of inherent conscience caught up with the victim of this desert Fagin. One night the rat reverted to type and carted away everything he could lay his jaws on at his immoral master's, and redistributed it among his erstwhile victims. That done, the reformed pack-rat departed into the night.

Anyway, packrats *do* tame easily, they are intelligent, and they make engaging pets. Also, they do all their trading at night. Which is the reason why you may not see them although you are likely to hear their rummaging about any camp or cabin.

16. *Amargosa Country*

A NATIONAL Park official deferentially ushered a dour gentleman from his car to the door of Westmoreland's Bar in what used to be the Rhyolite railroad station before the railroad was taken away.

He knocked.

"Whothahell is it?" Wes called from the darkness within, for the emporium was in the eclipse of mid-morning.

"The Secretary of the Interior!" The announcement was properly compounded of importance and deference.

"No better than the rest of us!" Wes boomed back. "Bring the son-of-a-bitch in."

Which illustrates the ghost-town proprietor's point of view, and seemed to charm the imponderable irascibilities of the then Secretary.

Rhyolite is probably the prize ghost town of the Southwest. In 1906 more than ten thousand people mined, drank, gambled, and otherwise existed there. Today, beside Norman Westmoreland (who bought most of the town at public auction) there aren't any permanent residents. The transient population, however, is considerable, as most Furnace Creek guests get there sooner or later—usually later, for the railroad-station casino is liveliest after midnight. Being in Nevada, everything is properly legal.

Between Scotty's Castle and Las Vegas there is no architectural gem to compare with that gabled depot. Now there are neither tracks nor ties where the Las Vegas & Tonopah Railroad so briefly operated, though one stranded, wheelless boxcar does sit where the right-of-way used to be, a static symbol of the rolling stock that was.

But newspaper clippings survive that give a notion of the fever which consumed those deserts back in 1906 when they were all but crawling with railroads. abuilding and projected. Even Death Valley was to be subjugated by the iron horse.

Gloated the *Bullfrog Miner:* "The penny-a-liners who write rot for the sensational newspapers will soon be deprived of their best theme. The railroad is approaching Death Valley and that awful abyss will be robbed of its terrors. . . . Where now lurk the red-handed assassins of truth and three-fingered outlaws with their guns, will soon flourish modern hotels, town lots and beer gardens. In fact, all the luxuries of civilization."

As it happens, Death Valley today is further distant from any railroad than it was in 1906; but at that civilization has done well by it, though happily bereft of those contemplated town lots and beer gardens.

Westmoreland's station is as sturdy as it was in 1907 when Rhyolite folded, though its interior is different. The men's waiting room houses the bar flanked by a gambling table and slot machines, its walls generously adorned with art intended for a strictly masculine audience. The nudes are plastered so thickly they literally seem abreast of each other. What was the

150

ladies' waiting room has become a place for banqueting of sorts, and the ticket office is a storeroom for bottled goods.

As much a part of the local scene as Wes himself, with his outsize Stetson, hirsute chest, and slippered feet, is Bolivar. Wes is an articulate extrovert and Bolivar a disarming exhibitionist. At the click of a camera this suave and regal red setter will assume a beguiling pose at his own special modeling place beside the steps, actually holding his head in whatever way best becomes the lighting of that time of day.

"Me," booms Wes, "I'm busy all the time. I'm barkeep, cook, chambermaid, and midwife. An' when there isn't any wind I blow to keep the flag flying."

Around Wes, I daresay, the flag seldom droops.

Rhyolite's biggest strike, as you read in the opening pages of this book, was when the Indian, Shoshone Johnny, sold his rights to the Montgomery Mine for two dollars and a pair of new overalls. Three million dollars in two years were taken from the local slopes and the neighboring hills of Bullfrog.

Still standing is the Bottle House. Its walls are made of bottles laid horizontally in 'dobe clay, the bottoms facing out, some of the glass turned vivid purple from thirty years of the intense desert sun. Already vandals have tried to pry out what might be museum pieces, as there is a great vogue for "desert glass," but the bottles break before they come loose.

As to bottles, beer at seventy-five cents per was about the most economical liquid available in Rhyolite. Water, seldom used except for cooking, was hauled from Beatty and cost too much to be trifled with for such nonessentials as drinking. Contemporary researchers assure me that children of a tender age were weaned on beer and liked it.

Other commodities beside beer and water had a ready market and sometimes it was necessary to invoke the solidarity of the Miners Union to discipline unfair competition. In 1906 this handbill was distributed around town:

The *Unique* and *Adobe* Concert Halls

ARE UNFAIR HOUSES

We request all Union men not to patronize said halls.
The unfair girl workers are:

Tessie Alfred	Kitty La Belle
Little Fay	Mazie
Skidoo Babe	Fay

signed by

THE CONCERT GIRLS

Withal, an illuminating social commentary.

Rhyolite has impressive ruins, as ghost towns go. Crumbling concrete walls of buildings that reached as high as three stories stand along the strip of present desert that was the main street. One skeleton is of the Southern Hotel, proud possessor of *two* baths. Banks and stores and offices once were where only ghosts are now. And, of course, saloons.

These last are well remembered by Cy Johnson who lives nowadays at Beatty. Especially he recalls the day he rode his horse into one of them and drank his liquor as he sat in the saddle. Local officers remonstrated. They ordered him to dismount. He said the hell he would. There was no law against having a horse in a saloon. Which, in truth, there was not. What was more, said Cy, he intended to ride out that door just like he came in. Which he did. And that was where jurisprudence caught up with him, because there *was* an ordinance forbidding one to ride on the *sidewalk.*

Cy isn't bitter about that at all. Through the retrospective rosy glow of fifty years it seems downright funny. So does the device they rigged up to fool highwaymen when Cy was driving stage. Important express was the gold they carried in bricks—honest-to-goodness gold bricks. Each was worth about thirteen thousand dollars and you kept it in a leather satchel up under your feet as you drove.

"We foxed 'em. A few times anyway," said Cy. "We had some nice phony bricks made up. They looked exactly like the real thing. You couldn't tell the difference unless you drilled into them. I'd carry one of these phonies in the satchel and chuck the real brick in the jockey box at the back of the rig."

Rhyolite was a lively town. Especially at times like the Fourth of July. Frank Grace, who has his mine over in the Keane-Wonder country, told me about the insignificant little man with the ancient horse who did right well on such occasions.

Drifting into town, the Little Man would boast about his horse. The runningest horse you ever saw. In the way of such things, there would be bets and a hoss race. The visiting horse was beaten, so badly folks almost felt sorry for its owner.

In the midst of the drinking that ensued, the Little Man, who didn't seem to know how to keep out of trouble, got to talking some more. Maybe his horse got beat, and maybe he didn't look like much himself, but bigod he was pretty fast on his own hindfeet. Anyone want to run him a foot race? Plenty did. He looked so skinny. By the time the race was all set the other contestants had consumed ample liquor and, though no one noticed it, the Little Man hadn't. He just kept busy placing bets on himself. Remembering what a poor showing his horse had made, everyone was cooperative.

The Little Man turned out to be very good indeed. He'd been a professional runner in Ireland. He won the footrace and a good many hundred dollars.

"He'd show up all around the country, he and his horse," said Grace. "Those who knew about his come-on game kept quiet. They liked to see the suckers get hooked."

In its brief heyday—it flourished from 1905 to 1907—Rhyolite was allergic to Chinamen. Which racial prejudice accounted for Death Valley Scotty's famous *al fresco* luncheon.

"I remember coming into Rhyolite one time when she was booming," Scotty told me. "The gambling joints and dance halls were going full tilt. I'd gone down there from the ranch, on a mule, and I got to drinking and didn't come back home when I was due. I had a Chinaman working for me and when I didn't show up he got on a horse and came after me. But the gang running Rhyolite said no Chinaman could eat there or stay overnight, and that my Chink would have to get out of town right away. They had the boarding houses all scared and they wouldn't give him anything to eat.

" 'Well,' I said, 'that Chinaman's got to eat.' So I went up to the district attorney's office and told him about it. He agreed with me that a man had to eat even if he was a Chinaman, and said for me to handle the situation the best I could, and he'd stand by me. So I took the Chinaman to a boarding house and told the proprietor I wanted dinner and I had my man with me and he'd eat with me and that he was a Chinaman. The proprietor said, no, he couldn't feed the Chinaman, but he'd feed me. I said, 'To hell with you, that Chinaman's going to eat.' So I went back to see the D.A. and told him the Chink and I was going to have our dinner together, out in the middle of the main street of Rhyolite, and for him to sit in the window

154

of his office, with his gun, and if anything happened, to stand
by me. He said he would.

"So I went out and bought a lot of dinner, and got it on
plates, and I took the Chinaman and we went out in the
middle of the street and sat down, and I had my gun across
my knee. And we ate dinner, with the district attorney sitting
in his office, with his gun, watching us out the window. I had
another man watching out another window with a gun, too,
but no trouble started and the Chinaman and I ate all right.
A man has to eat even if he is a Chink."

Rhyolite is probably the top attraction in the watershed of
the bitter Amargosa River, which is so seldom wet and ends
entirely in the salty floor of Death Valley after a geographical
contortion which causes it to flow due north after starting
south.

Beside the freakishness of the hide-and-seek river itself, the
valley, high and dry, is typical of desert country unless you
insist upon sand dunes. The Amargosa is the most easterly of
the four valleys with which this book is concerned, each ex-
tending approximately north and south and each more or less
parallel, the four of them gridironing the arid region between
the Sierra and the western borderlands of Nevada. Next to it
is Death Valley, then Panamint, and beyond that, Owens
Valley. The Amargosa's hills are for the most part rounded
and the scenery unspectacular compared with Death Valley
although all wide desert landscapes have their special charms
of light and coloring.

On the eastern fringe of the valley is a lookout called
Chloride Cliff, at the summit of the Funeral Mountains. The
steep drive and short walk to it are rewarded by a superlative
view of Death Valley, the tawny Panamints beyond, and

further still the snowy skyline of the Sierra sometimes visible all the way to the Minarets near Yosemite.

Farther to the south a main road leads from Furnace Creek in Death Valley, direct to Death Valley Junction, whose railroad, where the "junction" occurred, is no more. Its abandoned depot, by the way, serves a higher social purpose than the one at Rhyolite, for the two waiting rooms are used by school pupils who come from forty miles in each direction.

On that road one may detour to Ryan, and also to the ghost camp of Greenwater, which in truth is not much more than the memory of a ghost, as nothing at all remains to be seen.

On a main route south from the Junction you reach Shoshone, headquarters of State Senator Charlie Brown who "senators" for the whole huge district east of the Sierra. Beyond is Baker, on the road to Los Angeles, and it may be that the menu sometimes displayed there will strike your fancy:

Canape Vinegaroon

Loco Weed   Cactus Tips

Essence of Scorpion Tail aux Yuccas

Filet of Rattlesnake, Gypsum Style
Grilled Horned Toad on Toast, Fluorspar Sauce
Century Plant en crême   Creosoted Potatoes
Roast Young Gila Monster—Antimony Dressing

Salade de Prickli Pear à la Cinnabar

Chloride Ice   Cake de Cyanide
Fromage de Sage Brush

Talc Wafers

Cafe   Leche de Burro

In all that wide region the thing about a recent trip which pleased us most was learning how a local young lady as demure-looking as she is talented, is paying for her education in mining engineering at a state university. Between semesters, with admirable practicality, she draws good money dealing black jack at Harold's Club in Reno. I gathered her only concern was lest faculty members chance upon her. But any professor, I should think, would welcome a trusted student at the helm of the gambling game he patronized.

Close beside the road between Furnace Creek in Death Valley, and the Junction in the Amargosa Desert, is a remarkable cottonball cactus with one hundred and thirty-two separate heads. Each of the heads of this particular plant is about the size of a nail-keg, and all of them cluster together in a huge bouquet of gray-blue thorniness.

This rare horticultural exhibit, which has few counterparts, is guarded by a high iron fence. Hundreds of miles as it is from any considerable community, humans would hack off souvenirs if they had the chance. The small percentage of tourists who have such habits create injustice for their more considerate fellows who are content to enjoy what they see and leave it as they found it. Wild flowers, desert holly, artifacts, and anything resembling a fossil fall prey to the acquisitive traveler, despite rules, laws, and penalties, or the obvious fact that when the holly is gone from along the roadsides and other objects of interest are picked clean, this region, and any other, will have lost just that much of its attraction for tomorrow's visitors.

That fence around the cactus is a symbol of a problem. The reason it has to be put there is the reason why one of the most interesting areas of the Monument cannot yet be thrown open to full public enjoyment. One day, no doubt, when personnel is available to guard it as it will have to be guarded when people flock there, the canyon I have in mind will produce much wonderment. Substantially, it is an open-air museum. As things are, its exhibits could be carted away by the carful.

Here is a unique animal guest register of a Garden of Eden. A Californian approximation of Eden, anyhow.

Those first tourists did not write, but they left their marks. Their fossilized imprints were set down in a hundred places by a thousand beasts of other days. Slabs cocked up at various angles as earthquakes and folding left them, like stacks of building board and thicker blocks piled in disordered ridges, are the pages of the "register," preserved miraculously. Each one once was the mud on the floor of a lake or the surface of the shorelines. Millions of years ago contemporary animals walked upon those surfaces. Now those records are filed away where the sun and wind and rain left them undamaged, like reference books in the stacks of some great library, waiting to be read when man gets around to it.

As Donald Curry has pointed out, most of what we know about ancient animals is reconstructed from their fossil bones, left by the animals when they died. But in this prehistoric barnyard we have tracks which show animals in active life, going about their everyday business. A hunter can look at the tracks of a modern animal and know a good deal about what he was doing when he passed that way. And in a measure it is the same with tracks that are a million years old.

There is, for instance, a clear story in the footprints of antelope headed in the same direction, with fossilized, mud-spattered, and irregular deep imprints revealing their haste, while beside the tracks of the pursued, one sees the pads of a big carnivore. What happened on the muddy banks of that lake a few million years ago is pretty much the same as the

158

tale the sand tracks tell where the trail of the little mouse ends abruptly, and beside that terminus you see, on either side, the faint marking where the hawk's wings beat once lightly against the sand as he took off with his prey.

In that paleontological playground once were Ice Age elk and bison, some short-legged beast that resembled a wild boar, small and large elephants, horses of various sorts, many birds, and countless two-toed hoofed animals. And camels in profusion. Until the time comes that you may see those camel tracks for yourself, as more of those "volumes" in the tilted "library" are examined, you may if you wish, read a bit concerning modern camels who just the other day were in Death Valley.

For other camels—theoretically descendants, if you will, of these early residents—figured in the history of the region. In 1861, three of them helped make the preliminary survey of the Nevada-California boundary. Sharing transport responsibilities with twenty-four mules they started from Fort Mojave on the Colorado River near Needles, and in eleven days got to Resting Springs in the Amargosa Basin, and thence into and across Death Valley.

On the soft surface of the desert the camels' large padded feet gave them an advantage over the mules, who in turn fared better in rough going. One old male dromedary is credited with packing six hundred and seventy-five pounds, something of a record for any kind of a four-footed common-carrier. Despite their virtues, the strange beasts created complications. When Panamint Indians first saw the apparitions they were sorely troubled, and most self-respecting horses and mules bolted.

These Death Valley camels were no doubt leftovers from the lot Secretary of War Jefferson Davis imported in the 1850's together with some Arabs to tend them. One can picture the

159

sensation caused by the odd creatures and their burnoosed drivers upon the rugged individualists of the frontier. The venture, soon abandoned, must have had the flavor of a Gilbert and Sullivan operetta. Ultimately some survivors packed freight between Sacramento and points in Nevada, others resided for a time on a ranch near Tejon, and a few escapees reverted to the desert for a brief period of precarious survival until Indians and outraged cowmen caught up with them.

One day some astute innkeeper of the Valley may go in for camels again. I can't think of anything more apt to please certain tourists than a genuine camel-back journey through the dunes—complete with photography.

17. Around Stovepipe Wells

*I*N 1905 and thereabout there was considerable travel between the mining camps of Rhyolite, to the east of Death Valley, and Skidoo, up in the Panamints bordering it to the west. About halfway, toward the western edge of the Valley's floor, was a place where water could be found if you knew just where to look for it.

In the flat, not far from sand dunes with mesquite about them, you dug, and about eighteen inches beneath the surface there was water. Desert winds had a way of filling the hole with drifting sand. My friend Gustave Marsh of Lone Pine—who built the first trail up Mt. Whitney—drove that way in 1910. He said the water, once you located it, was "green and woolly." You bailed out the thick stuff and quickly the hole filled again with clear liquid.

Some orderly minded traveler finally stuck a couple of stovepipes in the sand beside the hole, which marked it very well. Naturally the watering place came to be called Stovepipe Wells.

So, too, did the nearby hotel started by Bob Eichbaum, a mining engineer who built the first electric-light plant in

161

Rhyolite, and his wife, Helene. Mrs. Agnes Bennett followed them, giving to this desert place in the shadow of Tucki Mountain, much of its special charm. After Mrs. Bennett's death in 1944, C. E. Fuller of Pasadena carried on with the property, which like Furnace Creek Inn was closed during the war, thereafter reopened by Owen Montgomery assisted by his daughter and son-in-law, Frances and Fernard Davis. The new manager qualifies as a genuine old-timer, for "Monty" was with the Borax Company for seventeen years.

The Valley's central, eastern, and southern places of interest are conveniently reached from Furnace Creek Inn and Ranch, which provide the focal point of diversified tourist accommodation for the whole region. At the north end of the Monument is Scotty's Castle, with its unique attractions. For the upper part of the Valley proper, all the area of its western gateway, and most of the show spots of the Panamints, Stovepipe Wells Hotel is strategically located.

West from Stovepipe the highway leads to Panamint and Owens Valleys, and the Emigrant Pass road to Ballarat and Trona by way of Wildrose Canyon. From the latter one goes to Telescope Peak, Mahogany Flat, the charcoal kilns, Auguerreberry Point. Nearby in the Valley are the Sand Dunes, Mosaic Canyon, the Devil's Cornfield, and dramatic desert panoramas.

Here at Stovepipe a specialty seems to be superlative sunsets, when the west beyond the purpling Panamints blazes with color and the receding light bathes the eastern mountains with pastel hues of lavender, rose, and gentle blues.

Those hills of Death Valley could indeed be the "rose-leaf mountains" of which Lord Dunsany once wrote me from another desert, the Sahara:

Some crumpled-rose-leaf mountains, from forty miles away,
Are luring me toward them through all the blazing day.

162

Some crumpled-rose-leaf mountains flecked luringly with blue.
They call to me and beckon as fairies used to do.

If lurid sunsets and lyrical desert prospects are out of your
line, there is a patch of homey landscape close at hand, reasonably reminiscent of the Iowa scene.

In certain lights the Devil's Cornfield looks enough like the
real thing to induce midwest nostalgia. The sand and soil about
them having been blown away, rows of straight-stemmed
arrow-weed stand up on their spreading roots, stilt high, so
that they have the silhouettes of hourglasses, and with their
tousled tops extraordinarily resemble shocked corn harvested
in the furrows.

Away from the Cornfield and directly behind Stovepipe
Wells Hotel is Mosaic Canyon, at its lower end a cleft carved
through a conglomerate of small rocks cemented together as
flood waters for centuries burnished them with sand and
gravel. The mosaic-like surfaces, often brightly colored, are
smooth as glazed china, framed by walls of taffy-colored marble.

In the foreground of the view looking eastward from Stovepipe are the dunes, rounded hillocks of white sand, their crests
curved in the flowing lines the last wind left, their slopes
rippled with permanent waves no seashore could contrive.

The dunes of Death Valley were placed where they are by
several factors and kept where they are by the peculiar air
currents the lie of the land dictates.

Sand for such dunes is provided by the weathering of two
types of rocks, sandstone and granite. The huge alluvial fans of
Cottonwood Canyon, draining out of the granite back country, is the immediate source of the material that made these
dunes.

The ground water-table of the Valley floor is shallow here,
as the drainage from Death Valley is interrupted by Salt Creek

163

Hills, which serve as a partial dam. Moist sand cannot be picked up by the wind, and supports such vegetation as mesquite and arrow-weed. The clumps of vegetation block the wind, causing small eddies, which create incipient dunes. North winds are deflected eastward by the bulwark of Tucki Mountain, and south winds are forced to the west by Death Valley buttes and the south end of the Grapevine Mountains. The resulting eddies tend to concentrate and keep in the vicinity any sand contributed by the rest of the Valley. The dunes change in contour from one storm, and one year, to another, but do not migrate.

One day the water from Cottonwood Canyon, eight miles or so westward on the flanks of Tin Mountain, will probably be brought to Stovepipe Wells Hotel.

A handsome souvenir of other days, found in Cottonwood Wash, adorns Monty's hostelry. That is Jake Abrams' lost express wagon.

Back in 1909, when the mining town of Rhyolite was petering out, two characters, who had thought up a scheme to get out of town not only cheaply but profitably, rented a team from Jake, who ran a livery stable. They said they were going prospecting for a few days. With twenty dollars paid down, they went, and never came back. A while later the team turned up in Owens Valley, sold at a reasonable figure by two travelers who reported they had lost their wagon in the mountains, and ridden in.

Jake got back his horses, but it wasn't until the war years, when Charlie Walker was caring for the hotel property at Stovepipe, that up Cottonwood he happened upon the wrecked wagon. Later, Dick Ayllvard, a blacksmith who had worked on it in Rhyolite, confirmed its identity.

At the entrance to Cottonwood are some Indian writings on the rocks, though pretty well vandalized by CCC explorers. Of greater interest is the mysterious map on the lower levels of the fan, about eight miles north of the hotel and just west of mesquite-covered sand dunes.

That is in the area where Charlie Walker had said we would find fossil clams as big as books. We didn't happen on the clams—though roundabout are numerous gray and white fossils contained in black, marble-like rock—but the "map" was plain enough.

The map, if map it is, is laid out with rows of stones ranging from the size of a large potato up to boulders bigger than a man's head. The principal lines often run straight for twenty feet or so, and then curve, twist and have lesser branches which sometimes bend around back to the main arteries. Here and there, but with no apparent order or reason that has been explained, are circles, often of larger stones, from a couple of feet to perhaps six feet in diameter. They might reasonably represent springs or lakes, if any topographic plan could be devised to fit them into.

From the top of neighboring dunes one can see large portions of the pattern, despite the erasures made by wind, minor erosions, and washes. In all, the rows of rocks occupy perhaps ten acres. One day, before what remains is further disturbed or carried off altogether by some sudden flood, making a drawing of this megolithic cartography as a lasting record would be a worthy project indeed, later useful in solving the mystery.

Some hold that if one studied the "map" as a whole and were able to fill in the missing parts, it would indeed be a representation of the region, or some other adjoining area important to the desert Indians in their seasonal migrations. Some such explanation seems logical enough.

If this Death Valley map is no map at all, but some primitive game—an aboriginal version of cops-and-robbers or musical chairs—or a maze of sorts, that, too, would be interesting to know.

Certainly too much labor was involved in laying out those rocky ribbons to charge them off as an idle prank. That may not be true of many petroglyphs found in Death Valley and other desert regions. While such writings sometimes had definite meaning, probably more often they were merely scribbling. An Indian was just as apt to doodle as he lazed around a spring or in the cool of overhanging rocks, as you and I in a telephone booth. It was fun to scratch characters in the soft stone, as natural to do as for a Down-Easter to whittle. And the mentally immature everywhere have that habit of scrawling their names on the walls of public places—and some pretty private ones!

Edmund C. Jaeger, authority on deserts, holds to the obey-that-impulse appraisal of much petroglyphy. There are, of course, many records, incised and painted, which have definite meanings and served concrete purposes, either to record journeys made and deeds done, or to point the way to water or camping places. While techniques in different areas and with different tribes varied, one conventional symbol was standard in the Southwest. That was the herring-bone cross-scratches spaced appropriately along a central line depicting the journey, each "cross-tie" indicating an overnight stop on the route followed.

Jaeger declares, by the way, that the region between "the Owens and Colorado Rivers probably contains more Indian picture writing than any equal area in the United States." He reckons it has probably thirty thousand petroglyphs, or incised rock drawings.

Around Death Valley the best of the Indian writings are found in Titus, Chuckwalla, Greenwater, and Emigrant Can-

166

yons, and there are many groups in the region south of Darwin and throughout Owens Valley.

As to our map of rocks, the modern Death Valley Indians do not understand or know who made it.

Actually, of course, the geophysical characteristics of such environments have changed even in a few hundred years, and still constantly change. Even in historic times many desert springs and waterholes have vanished and new ones appeared. There has been a like mobility of human occupation. It is quite possible, for instance, that not so long ago there was ample water where the map now is, and where we do know that an ancient Indian trail led directly across the Valley from Tin Mountain to the Funerals.

Often on the rocks used in those maplike labyrinths one finds examples of a phenomenon called "desert varnish."

The observing visitor notices the dark, oily "varnish" that coats some of the bedrock, and the cobble of the older fans. It develops on most of the dense, siliceous rocks; in general only the limestones and the pure white Eureka quartzite do not exhibit it to some degree. The varnish consists of a thin film of manganese and iron oxides that vary in color from a light tan to a dense shiny black, depending on age and thickness.

The formation of desert varnish has never been adequately explained but is apparently a process of solution from the interior of the rock and its deposition as oxides on the surface. Perhaps the heat and intense sunlight have a part in the reaction. The relative time that a stone has lain on a fan undisturbed can be judged by the color of the desert varnish. For instance, the small fans or cones near Badwater are mottled with patches of different shades of browns, marking flood activities at different periods in the past. The length of time required to produce desert varnish should probably be measured in hundreds rather than thousands of years.

167

What seem to me the Monument's two finest views are reached from the Emigrant Canyon Road. My favorite is that from Auguerreberry Point whence one looks eastward all the way to Charleston Peak (alt. 11,910 feet) eighty miles distant in Nevada. If you stand at Dante's View of a morning and at Auguerreberry when the afternoon shadows march out across the Valley from the Panamints, you will have enjoyed the visual superlatives of the region.

The Point, with an altitude of 6000 feet, is named for Pete Auguerreberry, a prospector and miner who with pick and shovel himself built the first road to the lookout. Born in France in 1874, Pete came to America in 1890 and after a stretch in the San Joaquin country herding sheep, as men from the Basque country were apt to do, transferred his interest from wool to gold and his locale to the Death Valley deserts.

On the Fourth of July, 1905, Pete and his legendary friend Shorty Harris discovered what came to be called Harrisburg on the flats you cross on your way to Auguerreberry Point. Actually, you pass right through the old camp, although there is nothing to be seen but the single miraculously clean cabin occupied by Pete until his death in 1945. Harrisburg, except for its mine—which Pete kept on working—has disappeared completely. What the passage of time has done to Greenwater, Skidoo, Panamint City, Ballarat is kindly compared to its complete elimination of Harrisburg. Those other erasures were partial. Of Harrisburg there is left not even a smudge.

It was Pete himself who found the gold that started Harrisburg, when he and Shorty were headed across the Panamints toward Independence Day relaxation at Ballarat. Impatient to reach the celebration, Shorty was not impressed. When all concerned had sobered up, the two of them shook loose from Ballarat just in time to stake out claims before the rush started by Shorty's loud talk had grabbed everything.

168

The new town was to have been named Harrisberry, a combination of the two men's names, but became Harrisburg, a word easier to say. Ultimately Shorty got ten thousand dollars for his interest, which, in the way of such things, he promptly spent, just as a year previously he had squandered the eight hundred dollars he took for his discovery of Rhyolite. Shorty said later he was drunk that time. Anyway, the purchaser passed on the property for sixty thousand dollars.

Beyond the site of Harrisburg and the turnoff to Auguerreberry Point is Telescope Peak, the top of the Monument.

Usually throughout the tourist season Telescope is heavy with snow, neither the final six-mile trail from the 8,500 foot level of Mahogany Flat, nor the flats themselves, being passable unless you include snowshoes or skis with your desert travel equipment.

For summer visiting, Telescope and the region round it is a fine target for an outing. Monument headquarters and nearly all its personnel are housed during the hot months in Wildrose Canyon, on the way to the Peak. A bit below the Park buildings, beside the Trona Road, are cabins open all year, with food, water, and gasoline.

In another chapter I have told how Dr. S. G. George and his prospecting party in 1860 had a hand in naming two of Death Valley's best-known native characters, Hungry Bill, and the doctor's own namesake, Indian George.

More imperishable still was the name bestowed by a member of the George expedition, W. T. Henderson, upon Telescope Peak, whose upward slope starts actually below sea level and rises to a true altitude of 11,045 feet.

In his book, *Illustrated Sketches of Death Valley,* published in 1892, John R. Spears describes the panorama first seen by Henderson, a fitting description, no more flowery now than then.

He climbed to the top of the highest of the Panamints, and standing there looked off over such a landscape as can be seen nowhere else on earth. To the west lay the Slate, the Argus, and blue with the distance, the Sierra Mountains. To the south rose Pilot Butte, the Calicos and far away the San Bernardino Range. To the north were the snowy White Mountains, while to the east, beyond the Funerals, were the Avawatz, the Granite, and range after range that had never been named. Between them all lay the valleys, yellow with sand and grease-bush, spotted with black lava buttes and brightened with the beds of soda, salt and borax, that gleamed snow-white or turned to mirage lakes, with dancing waters and leafy borders, according as the sun's ray fell upon them. The picture from that peak of the Panamints is not to be compared with any tawdry scene that needs the colors of vegetation to make it attractive.

18. Star-Spangled Gem Basket

ONE morning Park Ranger Sam Houston and I set out on the long bumpy ride across the alluvial fan that thousands of years of forgotten flood water has borne out of Cottonwood Canyon, with some miles of hiking beyond where the road ends—though it never did rightly begin. As we left Stovepipe Wells Hotel the last reminder called to me by Nina Conley was to be sure and bring back some chalcedony roses.

"I need them," she declared, "for the hounds."

Which sounded like throwing horticulture to the dogs.

A rose by any other name would have seemed as unattainable that coolish January morning, for even the first of the venturesome wild flowers had scarcely thrust green tips through the gravel and sand. And roses over there in the bare creased canyons beneath Tin Mountain seemed altogether unlikely.

But, of course, the rose wanted was the megolithic variety. A rose of stone. To be exact, one of those odd geologic posies sometimes found in a translucent variety of quartz, lustrous and lovely and shaped like a flower. Enough like one, at least, to justify its name, in the eyes of those who collect rocks and gems and similar souvenirs of the bare countryside.

These collectors are the Rock Hounds, as ubiquitous today as desert rats were in more primitive yesterdays. In the Death Valley country where prospectors and burros have become all but obsolescent, rock and gem enthusiasts thrive like the green mesquite tree.

In Wildrose Canyon where she and her husband have a pleasant stopping place for tourists, I came to know the leader among local Rock Hounds. She is Mrs. George Pipkin. Three hundred and sixty-five days each year, I surmise, Anne Pipkin thinks of or collects rocks and desert gems, about which she knows as much as any, and more than most. From her comes the information set down in the pages that follow, the briefest sort of introduction to a subject broad enough to deserve a book by itself.

Rock Hounds, in a manner of speaking, are a sort of modern counterpart of old-fashioned desert prospectors. But their quest is a hobby, not a profession. They explore remote canyons, climb mountains, visit old waterholes, talk with miners. While no corner of the desert lacks its special quarry, favored hunting grounds are mine dumps where the initiated find mineral specimens and gem stones obligingly brought out from tunnels underground.

Rock Hounds prospect not for mines, but for individual souvenirs of the desert they can take home with them. Instead of autographs or postage stamps or first editions these collectors seek handsome specimens, gem rocks that can be fashioned by skillful cutting, polishing, and mounting into articles like paperweights, table tops, bookends, pins, bracelets, rings. The breed is part of desert countries, and as plentiful as cactus and as persistent.

These rock collectors are of three classes.

The novice goes on field trips for the outing. He is apt to become a bearer of burdens, a sort of accommodating burro who finds himself carrying the specimens his companions pick up, especially if those companions are of the feminine persuasion and possessed of charm, which they usually are, for desert sun and setting are kind to pulchritude.

The second Rock Hound category comprises the amateur mineralogist who can identify most of the mineral specimens he finds and has a pretty thorough acquaintance with their uses and comparative values.

Then there is the specialist, the collector. He not only is versed in mineralogy, but also has lapidary equipment and the know-how to cut and polish the precious and semi-precious gem stones harvested on the field trips.

Nowadays there are many clubs and societies made up of enthusiastic collectors. Mineral clubs of Southern California often make field trips to the Death Valley region. Within a radius of one hundred miles from Furnace Creek the rich collecting grounds are well called the "mineral basket of the West." However hard on commercial mining the vagaries of the chaotic geology may be, they are satisfactory enough for Rock Hounds who seek handfuls where miners need carloads.

With Anne Pipkin of the Searles Lake Gem and Mineral Society we have made some theoretical collecting tours. Right on her own home grounds near Trona one finds hanksite, halite, sulphoalite, and gay-lussite, and moonstones, too, on the southern shores in the shadows of the Pinnacles. For fluorescent experts who do their hunting at night—these magical lights supplement the equipment of many collectors—a side trip to the West end lime quarry and the Ophir Mine holds special interest.

In the Slate Range, north of Searles Basin, are encountered

173

jasper, chrysoprase, and basanite, and beyond, in Panamint Valley, antimony and cervantite in the side canyons, and onyx north of the old Nadeau shotgun road at the onyx mine which lies in Sheppard Canyon. South of Ballarat is the Cecil R Mine, well supplied with aragonite. Farther down the Valley is Golar Canyon where lies a deposit of ophicalcite beside the road, assuming that the road itself is still there! Butte Valley, not far away, is a place for fossils, a specialized collector's item, the butte itself, with or without fossils, well worth seeing with its contorted conglomeration of ribbons of contrasting strata created by an uptilt and stratification of many deposits, including limestones with crinoids and replacements, jasper and mother minerals.

North and west of Panamint Valley is the Darwin country, an area rich in mineral specimens such as iron pyrites, limonite-pseudomorphs, and Iceland spar. In Darwin wash, below the famous falls, are chunks of pure galena, called "spuds," that eroded from their mother ledges and were carried down the wash by cloudbursts, their rolling passage through the sands and gravel fashioning them into the shape of Irish potatoes that you may harvest at depths of a few inches to a few feet.

In the northern part of Death Valley itself, a favorite camping place for collectors is Mesquite Springs near the Sand Dunes. Thence the territory back of Tin Mountain may be explored for limestone concretions, travertine, and aragonite. In the heart of the Valley in Furnace Creek Wash and actually in sight of the Inn itself, are fossils, mostly of the receptaculite species. Easterly at the borax mine at Ryan, colemanite and meyerhofferite crystals are available but it is in the Owls Head Mountains to the South that the richest hunting grounds are found, and these lie outside the Monument so that there are no restrictions on collecting other than decent respect for private property. Bordered sixty miles to the west by the Rand district, and some sixty miles southward by Barstow and the Calico Mountains, this region is indeed a Rock Hound's paradise offering the skillful collector a really extraordinary variety of specimens that include tungsten, copper, jasper, agate, calcite, honey opal, fern rock, fossils, turquoise, obsidian chalcedony, nodules, geodes, and much besides.

Which, of course, is but the barest indication of the field day a rock collector can enjoy in many regions of the Death Valley country. Perhaps before long an articulate Rock Hound will produce a book telling exactly where to go, what to collect, and how to handle the specimens secured. There is an audience for such an overall volume. At present the best information I know, which from month to month covers various facets of the subject, is to be found in the rock collector's pages of *Desert Magazine.*

Beside the gems of desert lands, their gems of the sky, the stars have a way of comporting themselves with a very special brilliance.

J. B. Priestley wrote of Arizona, a part of the New World he found very old indeed, that it was a place of geology by day and astronomy at night.

All deserts are that way. And nowhere do the stars seem nearer, or burn brighter, than in Death Valley.

At Stovepipe Wells Hotel is a lady who loves stars. Through the dry thin air of the Valley and its cloudless skies, Nina Conley—the same who wanted the chalcedony roses—has been studying the velvety heavens so long that I think she regards her Death Valley stars as special friends, somehow different from ordinary stars elsewhere. She has a telescope and

175

proper pictures, and often of an evening when the desert is coolly still and the empyrean is electric with its own lights, she talks about her friends.

The January night Nina and I discussed the stars, the full moon—you can't know how vastly full a full moon can be until you see it smothering a desertscape in its almost daylight beams—sat in the sky exactly between Mars and Saturn, for it was an early hour. Later, the pattern was quite different.

"It's forever changing," said my desert astronomer. "Every hour, every night, every month."

"As much as the hotel's guest list, eh?"

She said that was true. "They're tourists, too, those stars. In October some of the summer constellations are checking out in the west. Then the Big Dipper seems to be resting on the crest of the Grapevine Range while waiting to receive the contents of the Little Dipper which appears to be pouring into it. Friendly Arcturus, just thirty degrees from the handle of the dipper, is blinking farewell, not to return to the evening sky until May. Only the sparkling diamonds in Scorpio's tail can be seen as its heart, red Antares, has already disappeared behind the Panamint Mountains with Sagittarius the Archer in pursuit."

For my friend the shifting pageant of the heavens was as real as any human migrations.

"In those first late autumn weeks when we come back to the Valley," she continued, "directly overhead is the blue-white diamond of the sky, Vega, together with Deneb in Cygnus the Swan, and Altair in Aquila. They adorn the western sky until March when they bow out of the picture for a five months' vacation."

Midsummer, we agreed, is not the time for Death Valley star-gazing.

176

"The next arrivals are the constellations Pisces, Aquarius, the Square of Pegasus, the many interesting personalities in Andromeda, the unstable Algol in Perseus and Mira in Cetus. They all pop up with amazing suddenness from behind the Funeral Range, and in November the Pleiades, too.

"During November and December Orion becomes a familiar figure in the evening sky, rising a little earlier each evening, until during the week on each side of New Year's Day he appears in the east just as daylight fades. In February he stands erect in the south at nine o'clock in the evening. In March and April he is rushing furiously down the western sky after Taurus and the Pleiades and as we close the hotel the first of May we see no more of him until fall.

"Northeast of Orion are the heavenly twins, Castor and Pollux in Gemini, and now in January the twins have as house guests two of the nomads of the sky, Mars and Saturn. Early in January Sirius makes his entrance, the brightest star in the heavens, following at the heels of Orion in his journey across the skies.

"In this bright procession is Procyon, the smaller Dog Star, ready for the hunt. Betelgeuse, Procyon, and Sirius form a conspicuous triangle which assists in recognizing them. In February, following this galaxy of brilliants, is Regulus at the end of the handle in the Sickle. Also we have a brief glimpse of Canopus, that charmer from the Southern Hemisphere whose appearance is almost cut from a Stovepipe audience by the peak of Old Tucki jutting out of the Panamint Range."

For the mountains surrounding Death Valley frame even the pictures of the heavens, just as they condition every aspect of its odd world and all that white men have done and found within it since first in 1849 they tried disastrously to scale rather than go around them.

19. Panamint Valley

To the west of the Stovepipe area, over Towne's Pass, is Panamint Valley.

On your way up the great alluvial slope that fans down from the saddles of the Panamints, the state highway was a toll road not so many years ago, one of the last two pay-as-you-go roads in California. It was built in 1926 by Bob Eichbaum who with his wife, Helene, started the Stovepipe Wells Hotel. Two dollars a car, fifty cents a person, was the toll.

Beyond Panamint Valley the original road turned southerly up Darwin Wash, to merge with the old route over hill and dale to Darwin, and thence back to the present Lone Pine highway. With the increase of Death Valley travel through this western entrance, Inyo County bought out Eichbaum and the State of California took over, ultimately building the present excellent highway from Panamint Springs directly across the Argus-Inyo range to Owens Valley.

Beyond Emigrant Ranger Station (the official western checking point of the Monument), the Emigrant Canyon road
178

branches off to the south, on its way to Wildrose Canyon and Trona.

It was that general route which some of the first emigrants followed, the Jayhawkers who burned their wagons because it seemed impossible to take them farther, and plodded on afoot. Actually, they passed not along Emigrant Canyon, but through the next valley to the west, which is now called Jay-hawker Canyon. There they scratched names and initials upon a boulder. And somewhere not far from the route you drive, the little boy who grew up to be Indian George saw three of the strange people with hair on their faces, as he peered down from his hiding place among the rocks.

From the five thousand-foot crest of Towne's Pass you wind steeply down to the broad clay playa of the neighbor valley gaily carpeted in the brief growing season with Death Valley sunflowers, primroses, and pink mallow.

Panamint is a browned and bare desert, a smaller and less spectacular replica of Death Valley and scene of some of the region's choicest history. Telescope Peak towers about it. The ghost mining towns of Panamint City and Skidoo lie along its eastern skylines. A score of mines, a hundred abandoned shafts, and countless prospect holes scar the slopes on either hand and the flanks of the hidden canyons.

In the Valley's central part the town of Ballarat once flourished. It was born about 1897, twenty years after Panamint City—a dozen miles distant up Surprise Canyon—ended its uproarious career. Of that hell-roaring deceased camp its new neighbors sang—

> *Her picks are rust,*
> *Her bones are dust.*
> *It's twenty years*
> *Since she went bust.*

179

Another twenty years saw the end of Ballarat, too.

In its heyday Ballarat was not a mining town but a place where miners came for incidental supplies and major entertainment which last was frequent, sometimes painful, but seldom free.

It was among the ruins of Ballarat that Shorty Harris spent his last years. And some of his prime, too, all five feet of him. He loved the belle of Ballarat, Miss Bessie Hart, an ample lady over six feet tall who weighed in at two hundred and ten pounds and could lick her weight in wild men.

The crisis of that courtship came one day at the Ballarat blacksmith shop when Shorty was sharpening steel and the lady of his heart's desire was working the bellows. Suddenly, there beside the forge as he put a good sound edge on a twelve-inch drill, Shorty popped the question.

"Bessie, let's you an' me get married."

The bellows stopped. The rosy glow of the charcoal died away. From her ample six feet the belle of Ballarat looked down at Shorty. Not unkindly, but with an appraising eye.

She told Shorty he was a fine man. And a good friend. She liked him. But as a husband? No dice!

"You're just too small for a damn big job." That is recorded as her final judgment.

Shorty did not argue. He died a bachelor at the age of seventy-seven, in 1934.

Today Ballarat's population is chiefly old Fred Grey and Seldom Seen Slim who exist in a lonely approximation of exclusiveness in two of the half-dozen 'dobe shacks still standing.

Fred has been there fifty years. Slim is a newcomer with half that span of residence. His other name is Ferge, and he has a sense of humor besides looking enough like Abe Lincoln to be proud of it. From his place of business—he has rock samples, and no doubt for those who want them, some very nice mines —several thousand utterly unoccupied acres stretch to the several points of the compass. Where the way to Ballarat turns off the Trona road, a sign says:

Slim's Place
FREE PARKING

The mountains around Panamint Valley in earlier days were favorite hideouts for those who had irked the forces of law and order. Letters for such vacationists from society were left in that box at Post Office Spring.

I do not know if Mike Casey received such mail but at least he bequeathed to desert annals a tasty homicidal reminiscence.

Mike was well and unfavorably known locally. He owed a friend one hundred dollars. When Casey struck the jackpot in a lucky mining deal, the friend asked for his money. There were hard words about interest on the loan. In due course, following gun-play, the lender became a corpse.

But the deceased had the last word. He had left a will. The will set aside five thousand dollars in cash irrevocably pledged to whomever killed Casey. That generous bounty for manslaughter in futurity, unique among murder rewards, created a tense situation. I regret I do not know the precise outcome.

Among the current mortal attractions of Panamint Valley is Charlie Walker, who cared for the hotel at Stovepipe Wells during the War. Charlie is hospitable and gregarious. If you happened by it was his pleasure to entertain you. He was his own cook, but not dishwasher. Legend has it that when every dish and pot and pan on the premises had been soiled, Charlie would import squaws who in a day or two would get the shambles cleaned up and ready for a repeat performance.

Charlie has been prospecting and mining in the Death Valley country for a quarter of a century. Before that he was doing the same thing in Colorado.

I met Charlie Walker at Agnes Reid's one winter morning. We were just about to shove off for Death Valley when Charlie rattled in from the mine in his battered pickup. We had a bottle of beer and later the exemplary Reid kitchen whipped up a lunch for us.

Someone once told me Charlie looks like Dopey in *Snow White and the Seven Dwarfs*. The resemblance is superficial. To be sure, Charlie has a Durante nose beneath a mop of sandy hair, and the copious wrinkles bequeathed by desert years give him a certain elfin quality. But he is no dope. His eyes are bright, shrewd, and kindly, his mind clear and his humor keen and he happens to be a mining engineer, an assayer, and a surveyor. On occasion he may have the untidy look of a desert rat, but that's because he relishes his way of life.

Charlie has been, as he says, in the chips often enough. Latterly the going has not been so good. But I rather think he will stick to mining until the lead he's working takes him right up to the Pearly Gates. And then no doubt he'll try to pan gravel in the golden streets of Heaven.

Charlie says mining may be gambling, but it's fairer and more fun than the kind with cards and dice.

"The difference between a faro game and gold mining," he contends, "is that with mining if you come out ahead someone working for the house doesn't give you a Mickey Finn and take away your winnings."

Which reminded both of us of the tale about the starry-eyed minister who came to Panamint in the rough days, hell-bent on reform. First thing, he planned a big revival, and then a church. One of the town's toughest citizens turned his barroom over for the opening services. What's more, that saloonkeeper headed a subscription list with a hundred-dollar donation. With that example, everyone in town came through. By the end of the second day the happy reformer had three thousand dollars in cash and many reliable promises. That night he was bopped with a local approximation of a blackjack and relieved of the cash.

History has it that it was the minister's original benefactor who got the three thousand dollars. On his investment of one hundred dollars that was good increment, even for Panamint.

"Someone else would have taken it if I hadn't," was his comment. Actually, he used much of it for good works in the nature of a very fine party he threw. Also, he generously equipped the departing divine with a stage ticket to Baker and one hundred dollars for expenses.

Charlie thinks Death Valley ought to be played up as a fishing resort.

"What you're most after when you go fishing," he says, "is to have a rest and be away from worries. The Valley's perfect for that. Your fly won't get caught in the willows. You won't get your feet wet or get tuckered out chasing along some danged stream to find a better pool. An' there'll be no fish to clean."

With that sound philosophy aired, we got around to drawing maps. At least he did. One sketch demonstrated just how to get to La Moigne's grave, the place where the sailor-turned-prospector tied his mules to a mesquite bush and then lay down and died. Considerably later his bones, and the bones of the mules who never managed to break loose, were found. He also showed us the location of the Indian map near Stove-

183

pipe Wells, which we found; and the fossil clams, which we didn't.

Mrs. Reid that day had two lovely baskets just woven by Rosie Nobles, a squaw over at Darwin. Their colors were made mostly from roots, with an especially lovely maroon coming from the quill of a finch.

A friend of Mrs. Reid's once wrote asking that she get Rosie to make a basket with a design of birds. In due course Rosie sent Mrs. Reid a message saying the job was done. "Bird basket finished," the message said. "There are no birds. There are elephants."

Why the switch to elephants no one knew. Charlie thought Rosie might have seen some Republican campaign literature.

As we finished our maps and our meal, Florence Piver, Mrs. Reid's daughter, said something about using the leftover batter for a couple of outsize hotcakes for the burros. It appeared they'd stick their heads right in the kitchen window if encouraged.

"Plenty burros 'round here." Charlie Walker shook his own sandy mane.

"Too many," Agnes Reid added. "Twenty-seven of them right up there in the canyon."

"Effete," said Charlie. "That's what they are."

"Effete burros?"

"Exactly. Too damn civilized for their own good. And tricky."

Those burros—Charlie said—even expect their drinks to be brought to them. They're so lazy they won't go a couple of miles to the waterhole as their ancestors did. Their newfangled notions certainly raise hob with the water system.

How come? I asked.

A two-inch iron pipe leads from a spring to the mine, where Charlie occupies himself, mostly laid along the top of the ground. The burros are so spoiled by modern conveniences they want their refreshment delivered right where they are.

"They kick hell out of the pipe," Charlie explained. "It's old pipe and busts easy. You'll see a burro with his mug up against one of those leaks he's made, guzzling."

Charlie assured me one story I'd heard about the burros and the pipes was dubious. That more elaborate creation alleged that the burros would *unscrew* the pipes. One would hold a length of pipe in his iron jaws so that it would not turn, the way a human does with a monkey-wrench, while his partner twisted the adjoining pipe until the coupling came apart.

"That," declared Charlie, "sounds like an exaggeration. I never saw the burros unscrew two pieces of pipe. But," he added judiciously, "I wouldn't be surprised it's been done."

"And," he chuckled at the memory, "one time I saw a burro get mighty surprised. That pipe line lies right on top of the ground. The day I'm thinkin' of the thermometer was about a hundred and twenty degrees. Well, the burro knocked a hole in the old pipe, all right, but when he put his mouth down to drink, it damn near scalded him. *Steam,* that's what came out."

The loveliest single feature of Panamint Valley is Darwin Falls.

The three-mile pipe line from Mrs. Reid's roadside inn leads to it. So does the highway toward Lone Pine, from which you swing off to follow a dry wash, beyond where the old road cuts across the hills to Darwin.

The first time I went there, approaching a cul-de-sac at the end of the blind canyon, our rocky way was close beside a rivulet of water trickling unexpectedly out upon the thirsty sand.

Where the road, such as it was, ended, we left Petunia, our

ubiquitous Ford pickup, and clambered among the boulders along the tiny stream that expanded as we followed it.

Shortly the canyon between sheer rock walls tightened to a mere cleft perhaps thirty feet wide. From a shelf above, the friendly water rollicked over a picture-book falls. And exactly as one would have it, beside the falls, where the light spray sprinkled them, was a pair of slate-gray water ouzels, pert birds with a lively song resembling that of a brown thrasher, happily at home in the shadowed dampness of this surprising sanctuary.

Beyond and above this lower fall was another miniature cataract tumbling miraculously from the base of dry rock, rimmed above with limitless thirsty desert.

There, too, are the frogs who sing, their performance reserved for the later, warmer months. The first I knew of them was from Aurelia MacLean who heard the frog chorus, and saw its virtuosos one April some years ago when she and her husband camped at the Falls.

"First," said Mrs. MacLean, "there was a whistling in the willows just below us, so very human we lay in our bedrolls and whistled back. Then we called. But the people we hailed never answered. After a bit of silence there was more whistling and then a sort of full-throated song. I never imagined frogs could be so vocal. And skillful. Positively, they sang a scale!"

With flashlights they located members of the chorus who weren't a bit bashful but rather seemed to enjoy the spotlights turned upon them. The pouch below their throats was puffed out into balloons as large as the frogs themselves. On such occasions—we read later—the lady frogs remain silent and deflated, audience for their caroling consorts.

This place of surprises was named for Dr. Darwin French who first found it in 1860, on his second expedition to locate the mythical Gunsight Lode. In that year Nevada Territory was carved out of western Utah and tales of the Comstock Lode fired all California with the will to find quick fortunes of their own gold and silver. The Gunsight figures large in the mining folklore of early Death Valley. One of several possible emigrants is supposed to have picked up a bit of malleable metal with which he replaced a broken sight on his gun. Later, the material turned out to be silver. Somewhere on the western side of Death Valley one could pick up pure silver! For fifty years optimists sought, but never found the Gunsight.

Nor did Darwin French. But he found Darwin Falls and mapped other good water at Bennett's Wells and Furnace Creek, important contributions to the white man's growing knowledge of the region.

The first he named in honor of Asa Lee Bennett, and he gave the creek its name because there they found remnants of furnaces supposedly used three years before by Mormons to melt down lead from galena ore. Some controversy remains about the creek, as the summer temperature of the water seemed to justify its name without benefit of the works of man.

Along the stream in that sweet oasis, whose charms today are no less than when Dr. French first found them, is a slim stretch of wet meadow with alders and some larger growths, and close to the bank a garden of watercress. From this horticultural miracle, there on the fringe of our driest, hottest desert, we gathered a dripping boxful of lush cress, a gift for friends in Death Valley.

In earlier days, before a fire destroyed all her papers and pictures and her motel's main building as well (since replaced), Mrs. Reid had that famous set of photographs of the hanging at Skidoo, Panamint Valley's ghost-town neighbor. That was *ex-post-facto* art. One evening an erring resident,

187

who deserved it, was hung. Hastily. The next day the press appeared. Always willing to oblige, the citizens dug up the corpse, dusted him off and hung him all over again while the cameras clicked.

They were authentic pictures. So is the story about their making.

20. Ghost Camps

*T*HERE are fogs even in the mountains around Death Valley. Skidoo, one of the region's better-known mining camps, was found in a fog.

Up in the Panamints, not far from that other ghost, Harrisburg, the reasonably impressive remains of Skidoo are still to be seen. Actually, considerable gold was taken from its mines just after the turn of the century. A mill was built, water brought in. The population reached close to a thousand and the town attained the dignity of a post office.

As to Skidoo itself, Harry Ramsey and One-Eye Thompson stumbled on its gold while on their way to Harrisburg, lost in a fog which is said to have been one of the two ever occurring in that country. At least that time the unusual California weather did a good turn. Uncertain just where they were, the men rested on a ledge of rock. Before they left, it was evident they had set themselves down upon a gold mine. Or at least, the making of one.

Bob Montgomery—the same who had done well by himself, if not Shoshone Johnnie, at Rhyolite—joined in the creation of

189

the camp that blossomed where the discoverers had set down their posteriors and set up their monuments. The camp was doing business even before it had a name. The citizens were discussing that lack. They seemed choosy and nothing quite suited their taste. Then Montgomery remarked that he planned a pipe line to bring water from springs on Telescope Peak, *twenty-three* miles away.

Yes, you've guessed it. "Twenty-three skidoo!" That was the wisecrack of the moment. At once, and not because of any logic, Skidoo became the name.

There is not much else to tell about Skidoo. If you wish to see a typical ghost camp, see it. Getting there is easy, while reaching Panamint City is a goodly expedition, the hard last of it on foot.

I had thought to retell the story of Skidoo's famous lynching, having talked with some who saw it, though, of course, purely as observers. But as lynchings go, the affair itself and what preceded it, was complicated and its details difficult to recapture. After all, the editor of the *News* was on the ground, the story was his *tour de force*, and he it is who deserves the credit. Also, I think it helps to get the flavor of the time and place if you read for yourself that effulgent reporting, just as I read it in the precious copy of that issue of April 25, 1908, now preserved in the Inyo County Library at Independence.

That classical scoop occupied all of the front page, and more too:

MURDER IN CAMP
MURDERER LYNCHED
WITH GENERAL APPROVAL

———————

Joe Simpson Shoots Jim Arnold Dead
And is Hanged by Citizens

———————

The disturbance which has shaken this community to the roots in the past two days, opened on Sunday morning last, when Joe Simpson, familiarly known as Joe "Hootch" (that being his favorite beverage) held up the Southern Calif. Bank here, for the nimble sum of twenty dollars, that being the sum of his immediate need. He was overpowered before he could collect, and his gun was taken from him. He returned to the bank (which is located in the store) again and became very abusive. Jim Arnold, managing partner in the store, finally put him out. Three hours later, he returned with his gun and deliberately shot Arnold, who was unarmed. He turned, and covered the banker, Ralph E. Dobbs, and would probably have killed him had not his attention been diverted. He was overpowered and handcuffed. Arnold died the same evening.

An inquest on Arnold's body was held on Monday, the jury returning the verdict "killed by gun-shot wound, inflicted by Joe Simpson." Some time on Wednesday night an armed body of citizens overpowered the sheriff and seized the prisoner and hanged him to a telephone pole. On Thursday, inquest was held on Simpson's body, the jury finding that "he died by strangulation by persons unknown." The body was disposed of.

It will go on record as one of the most remarkable lynchings that has taken place in the United States for many years. Joe Simpson, locally known as "Hootch"—owing to his fondness for the liquor known by that name, had been indulging in his favorite stimulant for some days and was in a highly inflamed state. Joe was out of funds, a condition not calculated to improve his usual bad temper, and to his disordered imagination the only practical way of getting it was to kill a banker. For this purpose he crossed the road from the Gold Seal Saloon, which he owned in partnership with Fred Oakes, and entered the Skidoo Trading Co.'s store, in which the Southern Calif. Bank is located. He immediately covered the cashier, Ralph E. Dobbs, with his gun and demanded twenty dollars under penalty of instant death. . . . A wild rush ensued and before he could carry out his threat, he was overpowered by a crew of citizens and dis-

191

armed by Dr. R. E. Macdonald and Fred Oakes, his partner. He became so abusive to everyone that Jim Arnold, the manager, eventually put him out of the store by force.

In the meantime Henry Sellers, the deputy sheriff, was on the scene with handcuffs with the intention of securing him to a telephone pole, there being no jail in camp. However, his partner and friends promised to keep guard over him until the necessary warrant could be sworn out for his arrest. He voluntarily went to bed and was soon asleep. His gun was hidden by Oakes. . . .

He was still under a bond of good behavior from the court at Independence, having shot up a hotel there on his last visit. Dwelling on these things . . . he armed himself with his gun which he had discovered in the oven and crossed the street.

He passed the bank counter and approaching Jim Arnold, asked, "Have you got anything against me, Jim?" and Arnold answered, "No, Joe, I've got nothing against you." "Yes, you have —your end has come—prepare to die," and with that he raised his gun and shot Arnold below the heart. . . .

In a moment the camp was in an uproar. . . .

Gordon McBain—stupid with liquor, and unarmed in any way, attempted to arrest Joe as he stepped from the store, calling on the others not to shoot. Less than fifty yards away, Doc Macdonald, kneeling in the dirt, with leveled rifle, again and again called on McBain to stand aside or take the consequence of the bullet meant for Simpson. From the other corner came the constable with his six-shooter raised, running like a deer and calling on Simpson who was moving slowly, crouching behind McBain, to submit.

With a sudden rush they were in the restaurant, where Sellers felled Simpson with a blow on the head, McBain still blundered between the constable and his prisoner. Simpson made a last effort to wrench his hand free, which still clasped his gun, and the constable, realizing that all would be killed in a minute, slipped his gun barrel into McBain's ear and threatened to blow his brains out. Nor was he a second too soon for Simpson discharged his last three shots at that moment, one bullet passing within an inch of Sellers' stomach. Before the zing of the last bullet had silenced, the constable had Simpson overpowered and his gun taken from him by Ben Epstein.

Simpson, handcuffed, but jubilant at his cowardly crime and at the hot fight he had put up, was taken to the Club saloon until a guardhouse could be decided upon. . . .

The lynching took place on Wednesday night . . . the body was discovered next day, hanging, and Judge Thisse advised of the fact. An inquest was held later in the day. While there was a general feeling of levity outside of the court, the investigation was conducted with due dignity. . . . One bystander remarked that he had been awakened twenty-three times during the night to be told that some persons had hanged Joe Simpson, and in his own words, "I was surprised every time." . . .

It is somewhat surprising that such an occurrence as a public hanging could be conducted so quietly. The only sound heard during the night was that of McBain fleeing from imaginary pursuers. Some time before midnight some person was heard to open the pool room in which McBain was confined to whisper hoarsely: "They're hanging Joe to a telephone pole. Run, Gordon, run like Hell." . . . It is generally supposed that he is still running. . . . He was seen on the following morning passing Stovepipe Springs in Death Valley, at a dog trot, a little lame in the near hind fetlock. . . .

Local gunmen are already in a chastened frame of mind. Would-be bad men as they bowl along the road on their triumphal entry of Skidoo will note the number, the stoutness, the great convenience of the telephone poles, and reflect thereon. It is a matter of deep regret, but it was the will of the people.

The next week's *News* said nothing about the aftermath of that working of the will of the people.

It is those photographs mentioned in the preceding chapter which tell that part of the continued story. It all was just a gesture of municipal hospitality. No one had the heart to send

193

away empty-handed and with their films unexposed those cameramen who came so far to do honor to Skidoo. . . . So, as I've said, they dusted off the corpse of Joe Simpson and hanged him all over again.

But even then, Joe's body was not to have its final rest. Cut down and reburied, Joe was dug up for the second time when a visiting physician expressed a desire for a nice human skull; on his third planting, Joe was minus his headpiece. So far as is known, he has since been allowed to rest in peace.

Some old-timers have their own ideas as to how the word "Panamint" came into being, among them Jesse McElroy of Lone Pine, who was brought up in Ballarat. His father told him the same story I have heard from others. When prospectors set out for the mountains friends wished them luck. It was like saying, "Good hunting!" Gold being the quarry, the send-off was to hope they'd find plenty of gold. "Pan a lot of it." "Pan a *mint* o' gold!"

That informal derivation is derided by the scientific mind. My friend Fred Hodge of the Southwest Museum writes me that it is all "a figment of the imagination." But he adds, "As a matter of fact, the name Panamint is uncertain of derivation." Apparently the terms "Coso" and "Panamint" were early in existence, but whether applied to a people or a place is uncertain.

For many years old Chris Wichts lived at the foot of Surprise Canyon, gateway to Panamint City. His notion about the name was the same as McElroy's. Chris, by the way, for a time was a saloonkeeper in Ballarat, when Jesse was a boy there. One night a community shooting got under way, with much indiscriminate gunplay. As a protective measure all lights were put out and most nonbelligerents rolled into dark corners.

Over the door of the Wichts barroom hung an ancient rifle, rusted into complete uselessness. Chris took it down, and during the balance of the fracas, while most of the population was taking potshots at whatever moved—not out of unkindness but because the mood was on them—old Chris marched stiffly up and down in front of his emporium, that antique gun on his shoulder, a memorable figure in the moonlight.

"Struttin' like a blooming general," Jesse described it.

The homicidal revelers left him severely alone.

However they may have come by it, the mountains are called Panamint and Panamint City is the name of the West's wildest and wooliest mining camp of later days. It was born, not too legitimately, in 1873, in a tilted basin at the head of Surprise Canyon, erstwhile home of the strutting Chris.

You can take all the good tales of tough mining towns and the counterpart of most of them will fit snugly actual happenings that occurred in Panamint City. Nature made it picturesque and man made it lawless, a refuge for individuals who had tangled with legal conventions in many ways and many places.

A barometer of the low regard in which "The City" was held is the fact that even Wells Fargo, whose daily diet was bad men, would have none of it. The environment was too well set for robbery to make the transport of silver bullion an attractive risk, so the express people told the mineowners they could roll their own.

The answer to that problem which Wells Fargo dropped back in their laps, was hit upon by a United States Senator. Two such solons, John P. Jones of Virginia City and William Morris Stewart, likewise of Nevada, were the prime backers and manipulators of this camp which was to have rivaled the Comstock Lode but didn't. It was Senator Stewart who got credit for the robbery-proof device: he had the bullion cast into silver cannonballs which weighed nearly five hundred

195

pounds apiece. As no one could run off with trinkets like that, the mines would ship a ton or so of this treasure at a time, nonchalantly unguarded in open wagons!

As interesting as any mental reconstruction of Panamint City in its heyday—with its one long avenue up the center of the narrow valley, its mill, the precarious trails that were the back streets, the inevitable district euphemistically called Maiden Lane, Sour Dough Gulch where the numerous dead were buried—as instructive, at least, is to visualize a little what neighbor cities were like in the 1870's.

That was the period when those doughty senators and some others, reeking with the wealth the mines of Virginia City had given them, were all but set to build another railroad from Los Angeles up through Owens Valley to connect Ogden with the Union Pacific. Such a road, with its west terminal at the Pacific where the great Rancho Santa Monica y San Vincente embraced Shoo-Fly Landing, would be a thorn in the side of the Central Pacific, whose Stanford-Crocker-Huntington triumvirate was somewhat unpopular with Senator Jones and his confrere Stewart. Also, that unrealized transcontinental system would have served Panamint City, and the storied wealth of Panamint City would in turn have fattened Los Angeles just as the Comstock in neighboring Nevada had made San Francisco rich. But, alas, the banking panic of 1875 killed off that ambitious project.

But in 1873 when Panamint City still was in its silver swaddling clothes, with the unconquerable Jones and Stewart at its helm, while they guided, too, so many other empire-building enterprises, Los Angeles was peculiarly receptive to such allurements. The town had by then a population of perhaps ten thousand. Though its municipal buttons were beginning to burst a bit, it remained a place of comparative tranquility, its streets dusty and untidy, its buildings mostly
196

adobe, with encroaching vineyards and citrus groves lending a pleasant rural air. Within the city was a horse-car line, and a railroad led to Wilmington, eighteen miles away. Daily stagecoaches made the trip to Gilroy, a rail-head south of San Francisco, and three times a week other stages started out for San Diego and for Prescott, Arizona, and another to Bakersfield.

But with all this civic blooming, Los Angeles looked with envy at San Francisco. The Bay City then had nearly two hundred thousand in population and was waxing very fat indeed from the wealth that poured westward from Virginia City and the fabulous mines of Nevada. Devoutly—as I have said—the citizens of the City of Angels hoped that the mines of Panamint would become, as their promoters promised, "better than the Comstock." Also with their own special brand of devoutness, the senators and all those wrapped in the silver skein of Panamint's fortunes, wished the same, not to mention a good many thousand investors who emerged at the end with tastily engraved stock certificates and nothing else.

Whichever way you looked in the California country, great balloons of inevitable prosperity hung in the golden sunshine. The year 1875 punctured most of them. Not, of course, that Los Angeles has done badly since. But the hell-roaring camp in the Panamints has.

If you wish to see the ghost of a mining town that was picturesque and rowdy, make the somewhat strenuous trip up Surprise Canyon to the 7,500-foot-high site of the city that was. Or, easier, one day read the gaudy story of its rise and fall in *Silver Stampede* by Neil Wilson. That is entertaining narrative, human and humorous, of Death Valley's most famous ghost town, and in addition, a case history that pretty well fits any of the boom cities of silver or of gold that came and went so fast.

197

21. Owens Valley

*W*EST from Death Valley, separated in turn from Panamint Valley by the Argus and Inyo Mountains, is Owens Valley, with the Sierra Nevada on its far flank.

An attractive access to Death Valley is by the Owens route. Through Lone Pine you can come or go from or to Los Angeles and the coast via Mojave, viewing as you travel gaunt forests of Joshua trees; bristling, bayoneted yucca that are shafts of creamy flowers in spring; the tinted erosions of Red Rock Canyon and ancient volcanic craters and black lava flows. And as well see the majestic skyline of the Sierra mount to America's highest peak, Mt. Whitney, as you follow along its granite escarpment. Via Lone Pine, too, you may continue northward to Lake Tahoe and Reno, or cross the mountains by way of Tioga Pass to Yosemite, and San Francisco beyond; or by Walker Pass, southward, to the Kern River and Bakersfield.

In this Owens country, in sudden contrast to the parched desert and its sub-sea-levels, you find in autumn and winter hunting and shooting, and later deep snows at almost any
198

altitude, with a score of ski lifts, snowshoeing amid every sort of Alpine scenery, crisp climate, and diverse accommodations. In summer there are peaks, trails, streams, lakes, and mountain meadows, for climbing, packtrips, fishing, and camping, and as well a dozen ports of entry to the High Sierra, as alluring a playground as there is in all America.

In a few pages one cannot give any comprehensive picture of a country so large and colorful. Those that follow offer only fragmentary sketches of some aspects of the history, places, characters, and conflicts of this neighboring hinterland that in many ways supplements Death Valley.

In 1845 John C. Fremont named Owens Lake and its valley. Almost anywhere on the Pacific slope you are apt to find yourself where Fremont pioneered—anywhere but Death Valley, for he never got closer to that than its far south end. He was as ubiquitous as Washington on his own home grounds. Only there were few beds for Fremont to sleep in, or houses for him to make famous.

Richard Owens, frontier scout and Indian fighter, was a partner in adventure with Kit Carson. On August of 1845 Fremont's third exploring expedition waited at Bent's Fort on the Arkansas River until Dick Owens and Carson, who together had established a rancho on the Cimarron River, could pull up stakes and rejoin him.

On the twenty-seventh of October, Fremont had reached Walker's Lake, to the north, beyond the borders of what is now Nevada. From there the leader took fifteen men to Sutter's Fort in central California where the discovery of gold four years later launched the bonanza of '49. While they secured supplies, the rest of the party, under command of Theodore Talbot and guided by Captain Joe Walker, proceeded southward along the eastern flank of the Sierra range.

Seven days before Christmas they came to the headwaters of a stream which they followed down to the lake into which it emptied but from which it did not emerge, a salty sink sometimes called "The Dead Sea of California." Fremont, in honor of Dick Owens, called it Owens Lake, and the name for lake and stream and valley since have survived. Of the many titles bestowed by Fremont this, and Kern River which the Spaniards called the Rio Bravo, are among the few that have not since been changed.

On your way from Death Valley to this region that Fremont found, the road winds down between the Inyo and the Argus ranges, the dry hills swathed in upholstery of brownish velvet, held tight about them by the creases of the canyons.

Ahead, westward beyond Dick Owens Valley and the salty whiteness of its near-dry lake, rises the sheer wall of the Sierra. From it, vast alluvial fans march down threaded by waterways lined with cottonwood that are green in spring and summer, pumpkin-yellow in autumn, mahogany-brown in winter. Those rivulets of color are like slim fingers reaching toward the gray granite backdrop of the snow-capped mountains.

Owens Lake, below you, is now shrunk to a third of its natural size since the waters of Owens River were diverted to slake the thirst of Los Angeles. Before the turn of the century two busy towns stood upon opposite shores, Cartago and Swansea. What classical scholar named it I do not know, but long since the original Cartago *delendum est*, and Swansea, too.

The steamer *Bessie Brady* plied between these terminals until one day she sank without trace. Perhaps when the lake dries up entirely, her bones, pickled in the brine, will be found. Eastward the cargo was cordwood from the mountains for the desert smelters and supplies from "outside"; westward, ore to be wagon-freighted two hundred miles to the port of Wilmington and thence by water to the original Swansea in Wales, then the nearest place equipped to smelt lead.

What used to be the blue water of Owens Lake now is a waste of white saline deposit. At Keeler and Bartlett, manufacturing plants endure bitter dust when the wind blows, and searing heat when it doesn't, while they go about their business of transforming their salts into commercial products.

In comparison to the three valleys to the east, Owens is green though not green at all as valleys are in Ohio or Connecticut.

Its hills are desert hills, their slopes good chiefly for grazing. But the floor of the Valley, when it has water, is verdant. Once, much of this was a prospering agricultural district, rich with fruit, potatoes, hay, and poultry. Now, except for restricted areas around the towns, the water has been taken away. That happened a quarter of a century ago, and since then much of the parched land has returned to sagebrush.

The story of this manmade drought is an epic of modern California, a winning of the West in reverse. The sad tale has been written a number of times, most recently by Carey McWilliams in *Southern California Country*.

Essentially, this neighbor of Death Valley is owned by the City of Los Angeles together with all the water of the Owens River and most of its other water supplies. Which makes for a unique situation the passing visitor is not apt to sense.

It seems only fair to say that Los Angeles would like best to see as little as possible development in Owens Valley commercially, industrially, agriculturally. It is an absentee landlord with negligible constructive enthusiasm. The less development and the fewer people, the smaller the likelihood of later trouble. The city's long-range desires would seem to be met best by keeping the Valley exclusively a region for vacationists. It relishes trout and deer more than residents and ranchers.

The adage of the greatest good to the greatest number may justify all that has been done. For a remote future, anyway. But at that, an observer cannot but feel that a better middle course of reasonable cooperation can be developed which will tend toward contentment today and less grief tomorrow.

On the east side of the road between Lone Pine and Independence you may see the cavernous fault left by the earthquake of 1872, the most violent of record east of the Sierra, though no doubt nothing notable compared to those of Death Valley's geologic yesterdays.

That temblor killed twenty-nine people in the hamlet of Lone Pine, changed the course of Owens River, swallowed cattle. Perhaps its queerest freak was moving a division line between two ranches. The boundary was marked by a straight row of trees that crossed the main road in an unbroken line. The quake shifted the trees on the west side of the road sixteen feet farther north, thus presenting to one of the ranchers that much of his neighbor's land. The trees continued to grow as if such treatment agreed with them. Whether the man whose land was conveyed by that Act of God sued to recover, I do not know.

To my mind the gem of all contemporary description of that pre-dawn earthquake is an obituary that delicately records the passing of a lady of questionable virtue. It adorned the *Inyo Independent* of April 6, 1872: "Lucy Blank and two Frenchmen, names unknown, were all found dead in the same room."

Like the Panamints, Owens Valley has a ghost city too.

In 1942 some ten thousand Japanese, evacuated from the

coast areas, were relocated at Manzanar, between Lone Pine and Independence. The official name of that unique offshoot of the war was Owens Valley Reception Center, built and operated by the War Relocation Authority at a total cost of about ten million dollars.

Toward the end of Manzanar's first year a director, Ralph Merritt, was installed; until the center's affairs were wound up early in 1946 they progressed on a reasonably even keel.

Tomorrow's archeologists may puzzle when they dig up catacombs among the sagebrush, that once were Manzanar's costly sewer system. But before that, other puzzles no doubt will be examined by historians concerned with the social and political obligations left in the wake of war and dramatically pointed up in this remote California country.

The war willed the western Death Valley country another community besides Manzanar which you will see distantly, at least, from the highway south to Mojave. That is the Naval Ordnance Test Station at Inyokern. The sailors have moved on to the desert in a big way, for N.O.T.S. is vast beyond belief. The area occupied by its laboratories, airfields, quarters, warehouses, and bombing ranges exceeds nine hundred square miles, which is just about the size of the state of Rhode Island. A good deal over one hundred million dollars has been spent there, and apparently plenty more is planned.

A neighbor to N.O.T.S., and perhaps easier for a taxpayer to appreciate is the establishment at Trona of the American Potash and Chemical Company. This isolated community of perhaps three thousand souls lies beside Searles Lake, a waterless, treeless, broiling, saline-infested region which William Lewis Manly somehow survived while on his way to rescue the emigrants stranded at Death Valley in 1849.

Today Trona is a place of minor miracles. Physically it is

an oasis of comfort and decent living, while spiritually it is by way of becoming an example of public conscience quite as much as of efficient commercial production. And all of it is set in the midst of as forbidding desolation as Nature could devise, not excepting Death Valley itself. One road, as your map shows, leads to and from Death Valley by way of Trona. With its improvement, more visitors who brave the hard country will get a glimpse of one of the most forward-looking industrial developments of the modern West.

Lone Pine got its name because long ago a solitary pine tree grew beside the creek where the town now stands. It was the only pine on the valley side of the bare Alabama Hills, a maverick that had strayed from the slopes of the Sierra. For the early settlers that lonely pine became a green beacon straight and dark against the tawny hills, a treasured landmark in desert travel. About 1870 the old pine fell.

John Lubken is one who can remember where the lone pine stood. John is a cattleman, a county supervisor, a bulwark of the community when bulwarking sometimes was rough business.

When John was young, Lone Pine was tough. There was a bad Mexican element and an equally lawless white gang. Seven men were killed one night, but mostly the murdering was spread out thinner.

The local killing most vivid in John's memory was the time three Mexicans, for good reason, were told to leave town. They left. A couple of miles south three citizens from Independence caught up with the Mexicans near Diaz Lake and shot them, feeling they needed it. They brought back the ears of the dead men as souvenirs.

A little later one of the three had a daughter born to him. The child had no ears.

204

"That," said John, "is gospel truth. I knew the girl well as she grew up. Where there ought to be ears she just had small holes in her head. The girl died when she was seventeen. I was a pallbearer. It happened exactly that way."

You have seen Owens Valley many times on the screen, though you may not have recognized it under the labels of Afghanistan, Utah, the Himalayas, Africa, the Andes, or the lawless lands west of the Pecos.

Death Valley figures frequently in motion pictures, and sometimes the pictures themselves are made there. But few locales in the West are more often used for actual movie making than the region around Lone Pine. The grotesquely rounded red rocks of the Alabama Hills, their sandy wastes, sheer cliffs, and eerie defiles, the backdrop of the Sierra and its photogenic slopes, have witnessed all kinds of goings-on in "Gunga Din," "The Bengal Lancers," "Stage Coach," "The Light Brigade," "Union Pacific," "The Westerner," "Wanderer of the Wasteland," and a score of Hopalong Cassidy and similar guntotin' dramas.

It was about 1920 that the first pictures chose the Valley for their location. Mary Pickford herself furnished the initial thrill to the neighboring town of Independence. And guess who graced the original Lone Pine picture, complete with redskins and frontier trimmings? No other than Fatty Arbuckle.

All of which makes the community reasonably picture-conscious. Four or five times a year visiting movie companies tax to capacity the pleasant Dow Hotel, a sixty-five-room hostelry which Walter Dow had the foresight to provide in a hamlet with less than a thousand population when he built it. You're apt to stumble across a star in any taproom, and the adroit facilities of Russell Spainhower are taxed to supply horses, food in the field, and extras of any sort desired, but

205

mostly in the cowboy and pioneer tradition. Then, too, on his home ranch Russell maintains a hacienda of sorts, very camerawise, which has been made to look like a dozen different places in a dozen different pictures.

Even infants often earn an honest dollar. One of the babies carried by a plodding pioneer mother in the picture "Brigham Young" was the one-year-old son of my doctor friend, Howard Dueker. The child's first birthday fell on Tuesday. The man in charge of casting postponed using this particular extra until Wednesday. The day wage of a one-year-old is eleven dollars; on Monday, aged *under* one year, he would have rated twenty-five dollars.

In the Mono country just to the north (you encounter Mono Lake on the way to Yosemite, Tahoe, or Reno) Joaquin Murieta, California's most fabulous bandit, used to hole up.

Some of the fables about him, and perhaps the facts, too, present him as a sort of Robin Hood, a desert highwayman who took from the rich and was good to the poor. In his way and in his day he may have been less reprehensible than a modern highwayman like C. C. Julian who robbed widows elaborately with his Leadfield mining swindles. Julian committed suicide in China. When the elusive Murieta was finally caught up with and killed, they cut off his head to take home as evidence of a difficult deed well done. Appropriately pickled in spirits, it was widely exhibited.

A name even more famous in the annals of the West figured, too, in Mono history. That was Mark Twain. Some of the most delightful improbabilities of his book *Roughing It* were staged thereabout.

It is too bad that Mark Twain never saw Death Valley. With its resources to work with, he could have wrought incomparable prevarications. But at that, on a more intellectual plane, he did well as an unsuspecting advance agent of Death Valley Scotty.

"Up at Mono"—Mark Twain wrote—"where it sometimes snows most any month of the year, when a man calls for a brandy toddy, the barkeeper chops it off with a hatchet and wraps it up in a paper, like maple sugar. . . . The old soaks haven't any teeth, having worn them out eating gin cocktails and brandy punches."

Two other writers peculiarly beloved by those who relish the out-of-doors, saw much of this land west of Death Valley.

Quite literally that was done by John Muir—who called himself "hopelessly and forever a mountaineer"—for often he looked down upon it from his Sierra. Once he climbed Mt. Whitney and spent the night there, although he had not even a coat and food was bread carried in his pocket. Memorial to that gentle man is the John Muir Trail which now traverses the crest of the Sierra that overlooks Owens Valley.

The other literary figure for whom this country meant home was Mary Austin. *The Land of Little Rain* and those other enchanting books she wrote of her California country are *her* memorial.

At Independence, its tree-lined side streets, white cottages, and lilacs oddly reminiscent of New England in this raw sagebrush country, you may see the cottage where Mary Austin lived. "None other," she wrote, "than this long brown land lays such a hold on the affections. The rainbow hills, the tender bluish mists, the luminous radiance of the spring, have the lotus charm."

It is from Independence, too, you can look off to the east and on a crest of the Inyo Mountains see a straight tall shaft of rock, like nothing Nature herself would have set there and certainly no man could fashion. They call it Winnedumah. The essence of the Indian legend is that a brave in other mightier days shot an arrow from where he stood on the slopes of the Sierra, across the breadth of Owens Valley. Where the arrow fell it turned into this shaft of granite.

It has always seemed to me that among the rarest phenomena of frontiers are their businessmen. The successful small-town merchant anywhere is something special, but in the very wide and very open spaces particularly fine examples flourish.

All the Death Valley country is long on distances and short on population. R. R. Henderson of Lone Pine, serving lumber and hardware to a region large as Connecticut, like many of his confreres, has developed technique of his own.

He has, for instance, a trick about small collections. Let's say John Doe has been on Rudie's books for an unconscionable time in the amount of $21.60. John is solvent but just doesn't get around to paying. Then one day at the postoffice he gets a notice about a registered C.O.D. package, with $21.88 due on it. John can't imagine what it is. Naturally, he's mighty curious, so he pays the fee and the package is handed him by Mrs. Tate, who has been postmistress for thirty-two years. Inside the package John finds a receipted bill for that $21.60, plus twenty-eight cents postage and collection charge.

"There's something irresistible about a C.O.D. package," says Rudie. "That gag always seems to work—*once!*"

This Mr. Henderson is a rugged individualist with certain elfin characteristics and on occasion a tendency to horseplay shrewdly tempered toward helpful ends. The way he handled that carload of bad lumber is a case in point. It was terrible lumber, half rotten and full of holes. In normal times no self-respecting mill would have shipped it, and it was unloaded before Rudie saw it.

Being too late to refuse delivery, the most Rudie could do

was protest. The broker in the transaction said he was sorry, but there just wasn't a thing to be done about it. You had to take what you got these days and like it.

But Rudie couldn't bring himself to like it. In that mood one day he encountered a truck going to Los Angeles, empty. He made a private arrangement with the driver.

The broker who couldn't do anything lives in an elegant home in Beverly Hills. Just at daylight on Sunday morning the truck backed up to fts emerald lawn. In less time than it takes to say grace at a Sabbath breakfast the truck, built for such maneuvers, slid its load on to the grass and departed.

The broker was unable to have the eyesore moved until Monday. As he had a good chance to examine the lumber, after his blood pressure had reduced somewhat, he came to feel so much the same way as Rudie did about it that ultimately an adjustment satisfactory to Lone Pine's imaginative merchant was had.

Nearly everyone who lived in Owens Valley a few years ago, or anywhere in all the Death Valley country, knew the Desert Padre. He watched over the spiritual life of a kingdom of God peculiarly his own, an empire no doubt tiny compared with Heaven, but larger than several Eastern states.

The padre's parish was all of Owens Valley, and Death Valley, too, and on occasion extended to Mojave on the far edge of its own desert, nearly two hundred miles south of Bishop. Sometimes on a single Sunday he would conduct Mass in Bishop and Mojave, and in Lone Pine and Death Valley as well. Nor had he an airplane, but a very earthy sedan, though often his foot lay so heavy on the accelerator, it all but flew.

Father John J. Crowley, born in Killarney, County Kerry, Ireland, December 9, 1891, died March 17, 1940, in an automobile accident. Beside the highway to Mojave is a monument that marks the place. Often friends place flowers there. Most appropriate, perhaps, is the silvery desert holly of the land he loved.

These were the deserts the emigrants came to in 1849 when they sought the gold fields and found Death Valley.

It was through the very region where the little monument commemorates Father Crowley, that Manly and Rogers brought the families that so nearly perished in the Land Afire. And by this same road those who survived of the Jay-hawkers, the Mississippi Boys and the others, struggled to the safety of the settlements.

Close to where the Desert Padre died is Walker Pass, leading across the Sierra, the very portal to fortune those emigrants sought as they set out from Utah Territory a hundred years before, singing:

Then ho, boys, ho! For California, O!
There's plenty of gold, so I've been told,
On the banks of the Sacramento!

APPENDIX

1. TRIPS IN AND AROUND
DEATH VALLEY

The National Park Service has listed, as follows, a few of the many interesting trips in and about Death Valley so arranged as to permit the visitor to see the most in a limited amount of time. These trips may be made in one's own car or with the sightseeing service provided from Furnace Creek Inn and Camp.

DANTE'S VIEW.—A half day, preferably the morning, should be allowed for this trip. The country along the way, such as at Zabriskie Point, is colored and carved in infinite variety. From Dante's View, perched on the rim of the Valley more than 5,700 feet above the floor, one can view at a single glance both Badwater and distant Mount Whitney, the lowest and the highest points in the United States proper. To the north can be seen a white mass of rock nearly 100 miles away, while the Avawatz Mountains lie to the south. Across the valley the comparatively somber Panamints, topped by Telescope Peak, stand out sharply in the thin air.

0.0 Furnace Creek	13.5 Ryan Road
3.2 Zabriskie Point Road	24.4 Dante's View
7.3 20-Mule-Team Canyon	

BADWATER.—Perhaps the most spectacular trip from the viewpoint of color is that down the east-side road to Badwater and beyond. A half day is required, the afternoon being the most favorable; hence it can be combined with the Dante's View trip to fill out the day. The side trips through Golden Canyon and Volcanic and Artists Drives should not be missed. At the Salt Pools a trail through the Devil's Golf Course leads to pools of concentrated brine. Nearly pure rock salt, covering thousands of acres, has been dissolved and recrystallized to form myriads of rough, pointed pinnacles from a few inches to more than 4 feet in height. On a still day the salt can be heard to snap with

213

a metallic sound as the pinnacles continue to grow. The Natural Bridge, while not spectacular, is well worth a visit. A few miles farther, at the edge of the briny pool that is Badwater, 280 feet below sea level, one stands on the lowest dry land surface in three continents and the third lowest in the world. On the rocky wall of the mountain, high above the parking space, is a sign indicating sea level.

0.0 Furnace Creek	6.0	Devil's Golf Course Road
2.0 Golden Canyon Road	11.2	Salt Pools Road
4.6 Mushroom Rock	13.3	Natural Bridge Road
5.0 Volcanic and Artists Drives Road	16.8	Badwater

HIGH PANAMINT.—This trip includes Skidoo, a resurrected ghost town; Auguerreberry Point, the complement to Dante's View, affording an unequaled view of the brilliantly colored eastern wall; the old charcoal kilns in upper Wildrose Canyon; and Mahogany Flat at the end of the Wildrose Canyon Road on the crest of the Panamint Mountains. A good trail from this point leads to Telescope Peak, 6½ miles distant.

0.0 Furnace Creek	44.3	Skidoo Road
17.0 Junction of Lone Pine and north highway (turn left)	45.3	Auguerreberry Point Road
	54.0	Junction Wildrose Canyon Road
23.0 Stovepipe Wells Hotel	61.2	Charcoal kilns
34.0 Emigrant Junction Ranger Station (turn left)	62.0	Thorndykes
38.4 Emigrant Spring	62.5	Mahogany Flat and trail to Telescope Peak

SOUTH LOOP.—This trip is an extension of the Badwater tour, continuing south along the foot of the Black Mountains, across the southern neck of the valley and completing the loop by returning along the west side of the Valley. Here along the line of the old borax freight road are a number of interesting historical points such as Bennetts Well, Eagle Borax Works, and the

214

graves of Shorty Harris and Jimmy Dayton. Most of the day should be allowed for this trip.

0.0 Furnace Creek	66.7 Bennetts Well
16.9 Badwater	74.0 Tule Spring
44.0 Ashford Mill	82.3 Devil's Golf Course
45.0 Ashford junction (turn right)	83.8 East-west roads junction
	89.8 Furnace Creek

UBEHEBE CRATER AND SCOTTY'S CASTLE.—The vast extent of the Valley is further appreciated on a short day's trip to Ubehebe Crater and Scotty's Castle. Standing on the edge of this deep, highly colored bowl formed by a volcanic explosion, one can look nearly 30 miles farther up the Valley. Scotty's Castle, which is privately owned, is a manmade wonder nestled in the weirdly colored rocks of Grapevine Canyon, a few miles from the Valley floor. It was built by Walter Scott, ex-cowboy of Buffalo Bill fame, and his partner A. M. Johnson. Standing against the dark sun-backed hills, with massive gates blocking the bridge that gives entrance to the grounds over a deep ravine, it has the appearance of a medieval stronghold guarded by its moat portcullis. Of concrete construction in provincial Spanish architecture, with towers and gardens, pools and plazas, it is as fantastic as the country around it. A guide service fee of $1.10 is charged by the owners of the castle.

0.0 Furnace Creek	54.0 Grapevine Canyon. Here left-hand road leads 5 miles to Ubehebe Crater; right-hand fork leads 3 miles to Scotty's Castle
4.3 Monument Headquarters	
17.0 Junction of road to Lone Pine	
34.4 Exit road from Titus Canyon	

SAND DUNES AND MOSAIC CANYON.—The dunes area near Stovepipe Wells completes the desert picture. Rippled by the winds, slowly changing in graceful curve and contour, they are best seen when the sun is low, at which time their beauty

215

is accentuated by deep shadow and sharpened crest. Mosaic Canyon close by is so named because its walls are partially formed by eroded and polished conglomerate, whose pebbles contrast strongly with the color of the matrix to form a striking natural mosaic. Thin slabs of copper-color limestone are found here that ring, when struck, like a silver bell. Nearly half a day should be allowed for this trip.

0.0 Furnace Creek	4.3 Monument
2.6 Harmony Borax Works and	19.0 Sand Dunes
Mustard Canyon Road	24.6 Mosaic Canyon Road
3.4 Gnomes Workshop Road	

GHOST TOWN AND TITUS CANYON.—This trip should not be attempted without first consulting National Park Service authorities, as the road is often washed out and impassable. The oiled road through **Hell Gate** and **Daylight Pass** leads to the famous ghost town of Rhyolite, Nevada, outside the boundary of the Monument. A turn-off on this road swings back through Titus Canyon and into the Valley. The beautifully colored amphitheatre at the head of Titus Canyon and its narrow, winding lower part are among the most spectacular portions of the Monument.

Road Information: Current road conditions and other information can be obtained from any National Park Service official or at Monument headquarters.

2. SUMMER TRAVEL

The following suggestions are made by the National Park Service authorities to guide those making trips into the Monument between May and October. If these suggestions are observed, your summer trip into Death Valley will be a pleasant adventure. Often the daytime temperature is only 100° or so, and in any case relative humidity makes even higher temperatures no more than uncomfortable.

1. *CARRY PLENTY OF WATER.*—A minimum of ½ gallon per person and five gallons for the radiator is advisable. Tanks of radiator water are available at strategic points along the main roads. Drinking water is best carried in water bags or canteens. Drink plenty of water, but avoid an excess of ice water or iced drinks. A little table salt in a glass of water aids materially in withstanding the heat.

2. *WEAR A HAT* while in the sun. A good grade of dark glasses is indispensable.

3. *HAVE SUFFICIENT GASOLINE AND OIL.*—Filling stations are 30 miles or more apart and are located only on the through roads.

4. *DO NOT DEFLATE TIRES.*—Pressure generated by heat is negligible, but heat generated by friction on a soft tire is not. Your tires *must* be in good shape and at least one spare is necessary. Check your jack and tire tools.

5. *STAY ON THE MAIN ROADS.*—They are patrolled by park rangers daily. Unpatrolled roads are posted as such and should be avoided.

6. *STAY WITH YOUR CAR.*—If trouble develops, do not attempt to walk any distance for help. Wait for a ranger or another traveler.

7. *WATCH THE TEMPERATURE OF YOUR CAR MOTOR.*—Don't "lug" your motor. Grades are deceptive. Shift to a low gear on hills if your motor heats perceptibly. Cool the motor, if it boils, by turning the car into the wind (usually the wind blows uphill in the daytime) and letting the motor idle. If a "vapor lock" develops, cool the fuel pump and gas line to the carburetor with water or a wet cloth, and let the motor cool. If on a hill, the motor can be started by coasting in gear. Don't blow into the gas tank as the gasoline will spurt back into your face.

8. *DON'T TAKE CHANCES, DON'T GET EXCITED, USE COMMON SENSE.*—Inquire of a ranger regarding current road information in the Monument, and heed his advice.

9. *REPORT* anyone else in trouble to a ranger or the nearest checking station.

217

3. MILEAGE TABLE

FROM FURNACE CREEK TO		
LOS ANGELES	via Death Valley Jct.–Shoshone–Baker–Barstow	306
	" Trona–Inyokern–Mojave–Saugus	277
	" Towne's Pass–Lone Pine–Mojave–Saugus ..	319
SAN FRANCISCO	" Towne's Pass–Lone Pine–Reno–Auburn ...	605
	" Lone Pine–Tioga Pass–Big Oak Flat–Manteca	468
	" Towne's Pass–Olancha–Walker's Pass–Bakersfield	534
	" Trona–Inyokern–Walker's Pass–Bakersfield	524
SANTA BARBARA	" Trona–Inyokern–Saugus	324
	" Towne's Pass–Olancha–Saugus	334
	" Baker–Victorville–Little Rock–Saugus	365
SAN DIEGO	" Death Valley Jct.–Baker–San Bernardino–Riverside	380
	" Trona–Atolia–San Bernardino–Riverside ..	360
SAN BERNARDINO	" Death Valley Jct.–Shoshone–Baker–Barstow	250
	" Trona–Atolia	230
LAS VEGAS, NEVADA	" Death Valley Jct.–Rose's Well	141
	" Beatty–Rose's Well	158

Bibliography

This brief bibliography includes merely a part of what has been written about Death Valley. It lists only the principal books which concern history, description, and human aspects of the region. It does not include technical works dealing with such subjects as geology, mining, flora, and fauna. Nor does it list the great number of articles, in popular and technical periodicals, which in whole or in part deal with the Valley. In 1941 the National Park Service issued an over-all bibliography, fairly inclusive to that date, which can be consulted at various National Park Headquarters and doubtless at many public libraries. Unfortunately a considerable number of the titles below listed have been out of print for some time, though the interested reader can secure most of them at any metropolitan library.

Austin, Mary. *The Land of Little Rain.*
   Colorful prose about the region east of the Sierra.
Burdick, Arthur J. *The Mystic Mid-Region.*
   The "mid-region" of the Southwest desert country.
Chalfant, W. A. *The Story of Inyo.*
   Detailed history of the region which includes Death Valley.
—— *Death Valley, the Facts.*
   Specific information touching all aspects of Death Valley.
Chase, J. S. *California Desert Trails.*
   Description of California's deserts, desert travel, and desert places.
Coolidge, Dane. *Death Valley Prospectors.*
   Sketches of picturesque people in and about Death Valley.
Corle, Edwin. *Desert Country.*
   Admirably told story of the region stretching from the Mex-

ican border to the ghost towns of Nevada, from the Mojave
to the Grand Canyon.

Federal Writers Project. *Death Valley: A Guide.*
A concise tourist's guide of the Valley, magnificently illustrated.

Glasscock, C. B. *Here's Death Valley.*
Entertaining description of Death Valley's people, places,
history, and legends.

Knight, Clifford. *The Affair in Death Valley.*
Fiction. Murder mystery in the desert.

Lee, Bourke. *Death Valley.*
A book about the Valley, its people, and its tales.

—— *Death Valley Men.*
Informal biography of Death Valley characters.

Long, Margaret, Dr. *The Shadow of the Arrow.*
Records of Death Valley travel and observation.

Manly, William L. *Death Valley in '49.*
The journal of the Valley's articulate pioneer; an historical
record of prime interest and importance.

Milligan, C. P. *Death Valley and Scotty.*
Imaginative sketches of the Valley and its most publicized
citizen.

Perkins, Edna B. *The Whiteheart of the Mojave.*
Personal travels and observations about Death Valley and its
adjacent country.

Spears, John R. *Illustrated Sketches of Death Valley.*
Journalistic account of a Valley journey made in 1892.

Wheat, Carl I. *Trailing the Forty-Niners Through Death Valley.*
Thoroughly scholarly record of Death Valley's emigrants.

Wilson, Neill C. *Silver Stampede.*
Detailed colorful story of Panamint City and the men and
times that made it.

Wolff, John E. *Route of the Manly Party.*
The ways followed by the emigrants of '49 in their escape
from Death Valley.

INDEX

Index

223